Mountain Lake Press

Our First 15 Years

Mountain Lake Press
Mountain Lake Park, Maryland

Mountain Lake Press
Our First 15 Years

Edited by Phil Berardelli

Copyright © 2023 Mountain Lake Press—all rights reserved

ISBN: 978-1-959307-32-7

Published in the United States of America

By Mountain Lake Press

Contents

PROLOGUE

Mountain Lake Press and its two divisions, D Street Books and Safehaven Books, constitute one of the smallest publishers in the United States. Its current catalog comprises only 31 active titles. Yet among that group reside some of the best and most praised books published anywhere in recent years. They include, for example, arguably the best book on driving instruction, the best book on international business travel, the best book in the West about radical Islam, and the best memoirs, respectively, about two careers in the Central Intelligence Agency and the life of an international opera star. The list also includes several excellent literary novels, among the most captivating in contemporary fiction, along with two compelling short-story collections. All of this was accomplished by a tiny but dedicated and determined staff. Given their achievements so far, who knows what new treasures Mountain Lake Press will produce in the years to come.

ABOUT MOUNTAIN LAKE PRESS

Mountain Lake Press was founded in 2008 by two author-editors with long experience, both of whom cherish fine writing – fiction and non-fiction alike. Our aim was to offer high-quality but reasonably priced books and multimedia products. We published our first title that year; the deeply thoughtful debut novel *Requiem for the Bone Man* by R.A. Comunale, M.D.

Then we published our first non-fiction offering, the fourth edition of *Safe Young Drivers: A Guide for Parents and Teens* by Phil Berardelli. In print since 1996, this renowned book on driving instruction has been highly praised by a host of experts and reviewers.

Also in 2008 we released the second and third books by R.A. Comunale; the delightful *Berto's World*, a collection of short stories about the youthful days of Robert Galen, the protagonist of *Requiem for the Bone Man*; and *The Legend of Safehaven*, the second installment of the trilogy *The Safehaven Chronicles*, which began with *Requiem for the Bone Man*.

In 2009 we released, on compact disc, the unabridged narration of *Berto's World* as well as Dr. Comunale's second short-story collection, *Dr. Galen's Little Black Bag*. The book outsold the works of 90 other authors, including celebrities and bestsellers, at the annual National Press Club Book Fair in Washington, D.C., that year.

In 2011 – after a year of editing and production – we published, as our first hardcover and electronic editions, *The Craft We Chose: My Life in the CIA* by Richard L. Holm. *The Craft We Chose* is an outstanding memoir by a legendary member of the intelligence community, and it immediately received rave reviews. We followed, in paperback and ebook, with *Clover*, the concluding volume in Dr. Robert Comunale's *The Safehaven Chronicles* trilogy. Just as *Dr. Galen's Little Black Bag* had done in 2009, *Clover* topped all sellers at the 2011 National Press Club Book Fair.

Also in 2011, we released electronic versions of *Safe Young Drivers* and *The Driving Challenge: Dare to Be Safer and Happier on the Road*, Phil Berardelli's audacious blueprint for reforming aggressive drivers. We then published Dr. Comunale's other four novels as ebooks. And in December, we debuted *Phil's Favorite 500: Loves of a Moviegoing Lifetime*. The title, available at first only in ebook form, presented a wealth of movie recommendations based on Phil

Berardelli's years as a TV movie critic and his lifelong love affair with motion pictures. Phil included many links to clips, previews and selected featurettes covering nearly every movie on the list, so readers could sample the recommendations instantly.

Breaking new ground in 2012, we released, simultaneously, the hardcover, downloadable audio and electronic versions of *Adventures in the Scream Trade: Scenes from an Operatic Life*. A frank, insightful and frequently uproarious memoir by Charles Long, the book presents a vivid, behind-the-scenes look at the world of opera made accessible to all adult readers. The author personally recorded the excellent and captivating narration. Also in 2012, we released downloadable audio versions of R.A. Comunale's five books, all beautifully narrated by Ron David, whose voice was familiar to viewers of the Discovery and History channels, and many other TV outlets.

And 2012 marked the beginning of D Street Books, our imprint for an eclectic range of electronic and audio titles. First was the ebook version of *The Caliphate*, a tense spy thriller by André Le Gallo, former senior intelligence officer with the CIA.

2013 saw our next new title and another audio version. *Among Enemies: Counter-Espionage for the Business Traveler*, by Luke Bencie, an internationally known expert on the topic, provided essential advice on protecting yourself and your proprietary business information while abroad. The downloadable narration of *The Craft We Chose: My Life in the CIA* represented the seventh addition to our growing audio library.

Our 2014 releases included two more André Le Gallo ebooks featuring CIA operative Steve Church; *Satan's Spy*, in which Church and Kella Hastings – his partner and significant other – attempt to thwart an impending Iranian cyberattack against the United States, and *The Red Cell*, a spy thriller that begins in downtown Washington, D.C., then sweeps across Europe and climaxes in San Francisco Bay. We also released, in hardcover and as an ebook, *Hillwilla*, a fascinating tale from veteran writer but first-time novelist Melanie Forde. Set mostly in West Virginia during a bleak Appalachian winter, *Hillwilla* will bewitch you from its abrupt opening to its life-affirming conclusion. The National Press Club selected *Hillwilla* as one of only two literary novels at its 37th annual Book Fair in November, an event featuring more than 100 authors.

The year 2014 also included *Global Security Consulting: How to Build a Thriving International Practice*, Luke Bencie's second and highly acclaimed book, which we released in hardcover and electronically.

In 2015, the Library of Congress selected all five audio versions of R.A. Comunale's novels, as well as Charles Long's narration of his superlative opera memoir, for the national Books for the Blind program, a singular honor. New print and electronic releases included our most important title to date, ***Inside Jihad: How Radical Islam Works, Why It Should Terrify Us, How to Defeat It***, Dr. Tawfik Hamid's brilliant analysis of the worldwide terror network; and ***On the Hillwilla Road***, Melanie Forde's excellent sequel to ***Hillwilla***.

In 2016, we released a unique and valuable resource for the nation's exploding population of senior drivers. Published as an inexpensive paperback and as an ebook, ***Drive On! Preserve and Prolong Your Time on the Road*** contains essential information compiled by editor Phil Berardelli and an exceptional group of journalists and experts.

In 2018, we published paperback editions of all of our hardcover editions plus two new novels by Melanie Forde. ***Reinventing Hillwilla*** provided the satisfying conclusion to her trilogy involving the residents of fictional Seneca County, West Virginia. And in ***Decanted Truths***, Forde explored her own ethnic roots in a sprawling saga about an Irish-American family in the first part of the 20th century. We also published an update of ***Phil's Favorite 500***, for the first time in paperback as well as an ebook. We released the long-awaited, updated paperback edition of ***The Driving Challenge***. And we released ***Small Wonders***, a most entertaining and insightful compilation of reviews and commentary by Jessie Thorpe, former book critic for United Press International.

In 2020, we released six new products, including three already in our catalog but not previously available in paperback. They included ***Phil's 2nd Favorite 500***, which continued his inimitable commentary on the movies; Jessie Thorpe's hauntingly beautiful novel ***Bolton Roper***, the saga of a young wife of a spy; and quality-paperback versions of ***The Caliphate***, ***Satan's Spy*** and ***The Red Cell***, André Le Gallo's riveting and exquisitely detailed spy trilogy.

In 2021, we released two updates of our perennial favorites; the 25th Anniversary Edition of ***Safe Young Drivers***, still considered the best book on driving instruction ever written; and the 20th Anniversary Edition of ***The Driving Challenge***, aimed at improving the habits of all adults on the road.

In 2022, we published ***The Quarryman's Girl***, Melanie Forde's deeply penetrating fifth novel, chronicling the life and ordeals of two Quebecois sisters who settle in Quincy, Massachusetts, in the early 20th century. We released ***Phil's 3rd Favorite 500***, completing Phil Berardelli's trilogy of movie loves. We also published ***Save Gas? Drive Safe!*** a practical guide to cutting motor fuel costs during this period of high inflation. And we released ***Mr. Bridges***, Jessie Thorpe's fine and acclaimed second novel, the deceptively simple, captivating story of a middle-aged man's crisis of conscience.

In this, our 15th year, 2023, we have published *In the Stars*, a collection of 60 reports and essays about astronomy and space exploration, culled from Phil Berardelli's days as Science Editor of United Press International, at the beginning of what the author calls "the Second Space Age." We also have released *Hunting Nukes*, the chronicle by Richard Phillip Lawless of his half-century pursuit, in the service of the U.S. government, of rogue strategic weapons programs by some of the world's worst actors. Lawless's meticulously detailed autobiography features a Foreword by former National Security Advisor and U.N. Ambassador John Bolton. And we have released *Galen's 30*, the third and final installment in the Berto chronicles by R.A. Comunale, who passed away this year after a long illness.

In 2024, Mountain Lake Press will proudly release *IMAGINE: Winning the New Cold War,* the planned first installment in a series of unique public-policy volumes. It is a most unusual book, and it involves an equally unusual distribution strategy. We are hoping the series will become one of the most important and popular on the topics we intend to cover.

Also in 2024 and into 2025, we will be releasing, respectively, the sixth novel by Melanie Forde and the third by Jessie Thorpe. *Guardian at the Crossroads* features yet another of Forde's unique female protagonists, but this time it's someone who possesses telekinetic powers. And Thorpe applies her formidable literary gifts to *The Human Drama*, which probes an ensemble of characters living in the suburbs of Washington, D.C., at the turn of the 21st century.

Further down the pipeline is *Phil's 2001 Nights at the Movies*, combining all three installments of his trilogy, with 501 additional titles presented as capsule comments – though not necessarily recommendations. Likewise, *Back on Earth* features dozens of reports and commentaries by Phil. Dealing with Earth sciences, the book complements his astronomy and planetary science compilation *In the Stars*.

Fifteen years ago, we began our business with an audacious, trademarked slogan, "Home to some of America's best books." As the impressive list of endorsements and reviews within these pages demonstrates, we think we have honored that commitment – and we will continue to work hard to maintain it.

OUR BOOKS

Adventures in the Scream Trade

A fascinating, unvarnished glimpse into this glamorous segment of the performing arts.

Charles Long thrilled opera audiences for more than two decades, performing on some of America's and the world's most famous stages and singing alongside some of the medium's greatest stars. Now retired, Long vividly recounts many of those experiences in this insightful, frank, and humorous memoir. Sparing no one, especially himself, from his acerbic wit and keen observations, he sheds a bright light into a world many of us respect and admire but few of us have ever encountered in such intimate detail. In the process he illustrates why the word opera, which means work in Italian, truly is a labor of love for so many who have given their all to their art.

Praise for Adventures in the Scream Trade

"Long's book surprised me by its earthiness and honesty ... He spares no one in his narrative, least of all himself ... [His] tone is downright irreverent, but it's beautifully written and easy to read; even the musical terminology is transparent."
—**Tom Glenn, Washington Independent Review of Books**

"This delightful insider view of the world of opera is much like some of the glimpses we get from rock-and-roll tell-alls. Opera singer Charles Long is a skilled wordsmith, and his narration adds verve and energy to his story. The result is a fun and enlightening listening experience. His elegant foreign accents add authenticity, with his best creation being, of course, himself. Particularly amusing is his colorful and frank description about being a straight guy in a world abounding with gay men. Also, his spirited account of the time he and his boss, an Italian restaurant owner, retreated to a back alley to settle a dispute over a microphone is amusing. Adding to the listening pleasure are gorgeous snippets of opera music."
—**Audiofilemagazine.com**

"Wickedly and delightfully atypical. He knows where the bodies are buried and he spells out locales, proclivities and locations. Long says what people know and dare not spill ... There are delightful scenes ... Buy the book. It's a delight."
—**Christopher Purdy, Classical 101 WOSU Public Media**

"Uncommonly candid and opinionated."
—**Mark Kanny, *Pittsburgh Tribune-Review***

"Companionably written in a bemused tone. It's full of stories like the time an aging tenor lost his voice in the middle of *Pagliacci*, and his "cover" (understudy) tried to sing the role from the pit while the older singer's wife urged her husband to try to belt it out anyway."
—**Bill O'Driscoll, *Pittsburgh City Paper***

"Music fans of all genres will identify with his trials, tribulations, and successes in the scream trade. Any reader who has ever screamed due to the slings and arrows of outrageous fortune will take heart in knowing that in Charles Long they've found a fellow traveler."
—**Chip Etier, Examiner.com**

"In the present day there is a dearth of singers of Charles Long's physical stature and vocal strength for the great Italian baritone roles ... One can only regret that his premature departure deprived him and opera lovers of the benefit of many more of

his stage performances. [His] book can be gainfully read by opera-lovers and would-be singers alike. It is well-written and contains much wisdom along with the anecdotes and stories."
—**Robert J. Farr, MusicWeb International**

"A revealing account of what might be called the engine-room of opera performance, with a no less interesting confessional of his often bumpy relationships and the health problems that led to his regrettably early retirement after some glorious years."
—**Bernard Jacobson, independent music critic, Seattle, Washington**

"Type in 'Charles Long, baritone' on YouTube and click on 'Il Balen' from *Il Trovatore*, and you will hear the finest baritone of his generation—vocal beauty from the thrilling top to rich solid bottom and everything in between. Then his career was cut short in one of the great tragedies of twentieth century opera. A splendid voice with consummate musicianship and enviable stage presence, he could have reigned supreme in his art. ... I'm honored to know him and call him friend and 'baritone buddy.'"
—**John McEvoy**

"Charles Long has written an insightful, thoughtful book about the inside track of the opera world, relating his personal path on the way up and then back down in an intriguing business. His interesting and truthful prose matches the artistic beauty of his magnificent baritone voice. I sang with Charles over the years, and he was a creative artist/actor who painted many colorful characters. All of this is reflected in his very edifying and readable memoir. I laughed and cried about some of the events that happened along his singing journey—including several I shared with him."
—**Carol Neblett, Soprano, Metropolitan Opera**

"Charles Long is a talented and dedicated singer whose work was always informed by a sharp and insightful intelligence. He is also a lifelong friend. His book is filled with charming reminiscences, backstage intrigue and truly funny anecdotes. To sing opera is an Olympian undertaking not fitted for the faint of heart. Chuck came to it on its own terms. Bravo for a clear and well-written account of a challenging life!"
—**Keith Baker, Artistic Director, Bristol Riverside Theatre, Bristol, Pennsylvania**

Among Enemies (and) Global Security Consulting

An invaluable guide for international business travelers, and a solid basic introduction for anyone looking to do business successfully on the world stage—both written by someone who has visited an astounding 140 of the world's countries and is a renowned security expert.

Each business day, some 35,000 executives, scientists, consultants, and lawyers pass through the nation's airports to destinations across the globe. They carry, along with proprietary documents and computer files, the latest in personal electronic gear. However, carefully watching most of those travelers—beginning the moment they arrive at the airport and often sooner—are uncounted numbers of espionage operatives. These individuals work for foreign intelligence services and economic concerns and seek to separate international business travelers from their trade secrets. To succeed, they use many time-tested techniques to lure unsuspecting travelers into vulnerable or compromising positions. They also employ the latest electronic means to steal business information often at a distance from their prey. This is the 21st century, after all, and economic and industrial espionage have become multibillion-dollar enterprises, utilizing a wide array of the most sophisticated means to obtain proprietary information. Luke Bencie is a veteran of this struggle. He knows intimately the threats business travelers face and how to combat those threats. In *Among Enemies: Counter-Espionage for the Business Traveler*, Bencie provides everything you need to know to protect yourself and your company from attempted espionage.

Praise for *Among Enemies*

"Thanks for writing and publishing *Among Enemies*! My VP discovered it at an airport bookstore and handed off to me. Once in my hands, I couldn't put it down. Your book has made a great addition to the information protection awareness tools we've developed internally. Plus you've validated years of what I've been telling execs about how to travel more safe and secure."
—**Bruce D. Cristofferson, CISSP, CISA, CISM, OpSec Officer for a Fortune 500 Telecommunications Company**

"A marvelous book! ... The most handy, the most accessible 'how-to' book to be aware of the threats that we're facing."
—**Frank Gaffney, Secure Freedom Radio**

"A must-read if you travel overseas."
—**William J. Esposito, former Deputy Director of the FBI**

"Packed with advice and information ... [Bencie] does not sugarcoat the human weaknesses that cause people to compromise themselves in the worst ways possible ... Electronic threats are covered in detail ... Readers who pay attention could thwart foreign [espionage] efforts and protect vital trade secrets ... *Among Enemies* is a must-read for international travelers and those who deliver foreign travel briefings and debriefings."
—**G. Ernest Govea, *Security Management* magazine**

"Great reading for spies and businessmen alike."
—**Remy Mauduit, former FLN Member, intelligence operative and U.S. Special Forces counterinsurgency instructor**

"The author really knows [his] stuff ... He covers all aspects of locking down your business information ... I have a new appreciation of the 'leakiness' of my electronic devices ... [An] easy read -- this one is immediately useful."
—**Reg Nordman, RocketBuilders.com**

"Indispensable and authoritative ... for every business traveler engaging in overseas business activities."

—Dr. Joshua Sinai, *The Journal of Counterterrorism & Homeland Security International*

"Required reading for the American business traveler."
—**Jack Lee, Vice President, Florida Satellite Chapter, Association of Former Intelligence Officers**

"The most updated account [of] the threats our American business travelers face when abroad with their intellectual property and trade secrets. [He] reveals, despite friend or foe, encrypted or hidden, your sensitive business information is at grave risk; but, this expert shows many ways to significantly reduce your vulnerabilities."
—**S. Eugene Poteat, President, Association of Former Intelligence Officers (AFIO)**

Global Security Consulting has been called, over and over, 'A must-read!'

With new security threats nearly every week all over the globe, governments and businesses are forced to take extraordinary measures to protect themselves. Likewise, espionage continues at levels comparable to the days of the Cold War—but many more players are now participating. In this environment, a new industry has grown to deal with these challenges: international security consulting. Drawing from military, law-enforcement, and intelligence communities, new private companies are springing up across the world. *Global Security Consulting*, written by a former intelligence specialist who has built a successful consultancy, provides solid guidance for anyone wishing to enter this glamorous but often dangerous field.

"Not only **a must-read** for operating your own business but a testimonial to managing any business with integrity and fairness."
—**William J. Esposito, former Deputy Director of the FBI**

"**A must-read** that can save you tons of anxiety, time and money."
—**Michael Heimbach, VP of Global Security, ESPN**

"**A must-read** for anyone who calls him/herself a global consultant."
—**Peter Davis, original associate, Bain & Company**

"**A must-read** for anyone interested in this lucrative field."
—**Gary M. Citrenbaum, President/Chief Scientist, System of Systems Analytics, Inc.**

"**A must-read** for all aspirants to this field and enjoyable reading for anyone interested in how international affairs, foreign policy and good business management are conducted."
—**Richard L. Holm, former senior intelligence officer and author of** *The Craft We Chose: My Life in the CIA*

"**A must-read** for anyone contemplating a profitable career as a Security Consultant and even for those of us who have been doing it for a while."
—**David Nicastro, President, Secure Source International LLC**

"**A must-read** if you are serious about building a world-class security consultancy in the 21st century. It is a tell-all from the front lines and is both entertaining and informative.
—**Vincent Volpi, CEO, PICA Corporation**

"Experience is key in this line of business, but you must survive long enough to use what you have learned, and this book is **a must-read** to study and profit."
—**Erik Lawrence, founder, Blackheart International/current owner Vigilant Security Services**

"Luke Bencie … offers a plethora of perspectives to help fellow security consultants establish or grow their global security consultancies or assist security professionals who are engaging a consultant."
—**Jay Martin,** *Security Management*

The Berto Galen Stories

Three short-story collections from a gifted writer with a razor-sharp eye on the human condition borne of a lifetime of hard-won experience.

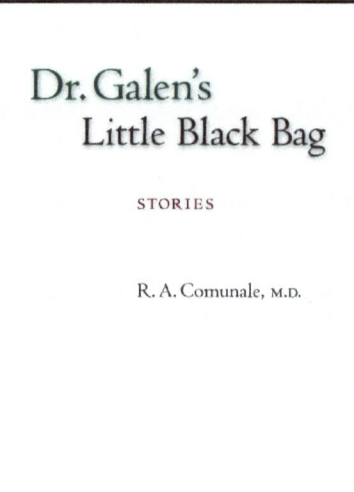

In *Berto's World*, we follow Dr. Robert Galen, aka Berto, as he traverses the memories of the tenement neighborhood of his youth and those that reside there. Meet the Mad Russian. Why does he always carry a meat cleaver whenever he goes to get a shave from Thomas the barber? Then there's Giuseppe Joe the Junkman who roams through a neighborhood too poor to throw anything away. There are the Old Guys, veterans of the Great War, one a radio repairman who returned home with shell shock, the other a shoemaker with nothing below the waist. There's Mr. Buck, the clockmaker, who shares a secret with his young apprentice. There's the Candy Lady, who isn't so sweet, and the little Jewish dentist who defeated the Nazis but falls victim to Cupid s arrow from a most unexpected direction. Be sure to meet Sal, Tomas, and Angie, Berto s pals who help him confront life s greatest mystery: the opposite sex. And above all there is his mentor, Dr. Agnelli, who along with a dead lady sets Berto along his life s path. Come and meet them and all of the unforgettable denizens of *Berto's World*.

Then, in *Dr. Galen's Little Black Bag*, we follow the man that Berto Galen has become, as he deals with the pleasures, traumas, and tragedies of life in the medical profession. Like Berto s World, it is a collection of stories, but together those stories create a portrait of someone who is deeply dedicated to healing even as he struggles to heal the hurts and wounds that he has suffered over his own lifetime.

And, in *Galen's 30*, R.A. Comunale's valedictory collection, we learn the fate of Dr. Robert Galen, aka Berto, who grew from a young lad on the rough streets of urban New Jersey, to a brilliant young medical student in Richmond, Virginia, to the bear-sized man treating patients at his unique family practice in suburban Washington, D.C. Full of passion and pathos—and vivid imagination—Comunale's third collection of short stories explores a wide range of human emotions and experiences, the full spectrum of the human condition. Afflicted with the disease now commonly known as Covid, the good Doctor focuses on both that difficult experience and further reflections on his half-century of medicine. *Galen's 30* presents 30 additional compelling stories by a gifted and beloved writer.

Readers' praise for the Berto Galen stories

"[*Berto's World* is a] brilliant second novel [after] *Requiem for the Bone Man*! Our protagonist, Dr. Robert Galen takes us back through his childhood and adolescence. Berto is living in a neighborhood rich with diversity and attending a Catholic School. We meet many colorful folks from the coal-man to the barber - all of whom have a story worth repeating! We get to know Berto's peers and his mentor in medicine, Dr. Agnelli. The story is told with such great understanding of human nature, humor, compassion - all the same attributes that make Dr. Comunale the exceptional physician he is! This is a must-read, a book that you can't put down!"
—**Betty Ann Yurkewitch**

"[*Berto's World*] was a Goodreads win for me ... Well-written with fully developed characters. When I can envision myself in the book and identify with characters, then it is a good book to me."
—**Linda Heath**

"[*Dr. Galen's Little Black Bag* is a] great read by a very compassionate, caring author. We have enjoyed all ... of [R.A. Comunale's] novels and highly recommend them to others!"
—**Bill Hoffman**

"[*Galen's 30* is a] must-read! A superb collection of short stories that will touch your heart and soul in the most surprising ways ... R.A. Comunale provides insights ... supported by his medical background, training and experience."
—**Cecilia A. Tabois**

Bolton Roper

A haunting debut novel from a writer with rare literary gifts and destined to become a classic.

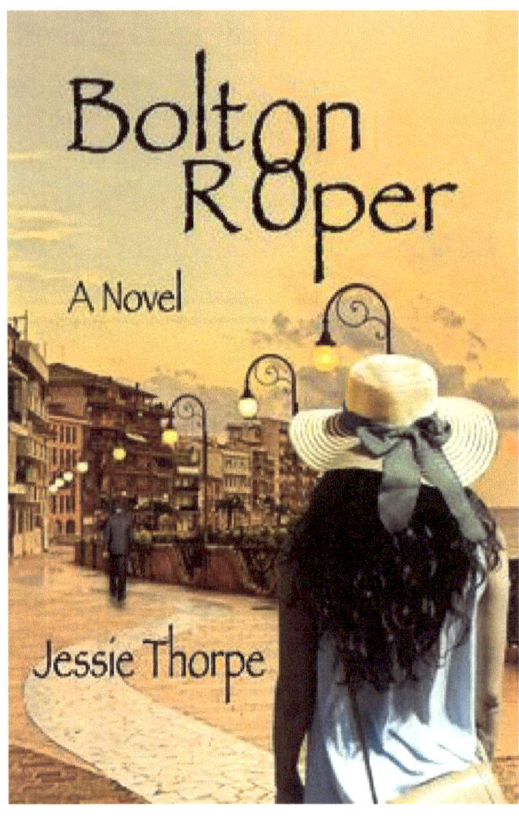

We first meet Brooke Roper, a beautiful American woman, as she gazes from her apartment balcony at the Italian sky above and the bustling street of Milan below. But her calmness disguises her severe inner turmoil. Brooke feels a growing panic about her station in life and her marriage to Bolton ("Tony") Roper, ostensibly an American businessman who is actually an undercover CIA operative. It is the summer of 1988, and the Cold War is winding down. But Milan remains a hotbed of Soviet agents, and Tony seems deeply involved in an increasingly dangerous situation. The plot unfolds via Brooke's recollections of that incident, of her interactions with her two visiting sisters—the oblivious Christina, with whom she shares several adventures in the villages and towns along the Amalfi Coast, in Naples, and in Pompeii; and the imperious Fleur, who startles Brooke into revealing the deepest secret of her marriage—and of her fierce, almost obsessive devotion to her husband, which leads her to the two most fateful and drastic decisions of her life. Bolton Roper is an intensely romantic, deeply haunting journey, both physical and emotional, amid the unique people and lush locations of Italy, within the banal suburbs of Washington, D.C., and at the family home within the bucolic landscape of a small Michigan town. Always vividly and arrestingly recounted, Brooke's reverie is the unforgettable story of the wife of a spy.

Praise for *Bolton Roper*

"Extraordinary and unreservedly recommended."

"A deftly crafted novel by an author with a genuine flair for originality and the kind of narrative driven storytelling style that will keep the reader's fully engaged attention from first page to last."
—Midwest Book Review

"A sure sign of a profound work, *Bolton Roper* shaped my mood for long after I closed the cover."

"Filled with poetic images that tumble, cloud-like, over an undercurrent of foreboding, this novel is not what it appears to be on first view – it is much, much more. Thorpe deftly explores the related themes of secrets and divided loyalties, which test every soul on both the quotidian and grand scale. Touring the labyrinthine thought processes of the first-person protagonist, Brooke, made me experience unexpected emotions and wonder at life's complexities."
—Melanie Forde, author of *The Quarryman's Girl*, *Decanted Truths* and the *Hillwilla* trilogy

"With *Bolton Roper*, Jessie Thorpe has placed herself in an elite circle of genre-bending authors capable of using clear, insightful, often lyrical prose to propel an exciting, yet deeply thought-provoking, espionage mystery."

"Thorpe gives the reader an almost intuitive feeling for place and authenticity. She is also masterful in creating a pervasive sense of foreboding … a powerful sense of momentum and inevitability as Brooke reveals the events that have consumed her. Even as we suspect from the beginning that things will not end well, Thorpe does not disappoint the reader. Indeed, this suspicion does not keep the reader from being surprised at several turns. Or from parsing the complexities that define Brooke—to parse them and see the future Brooke hopes for but will not clearly attain."
—Richard Samuel Sheres, author of *An Imperfect Certainty*, *Ingersoll*, and *Keeping Gideon* (a San Diego Book Awards finalist)

The Craft We Chose

A landmark memoir by a legendary member of the intelligence community.

Many books, fiction and nonfiction alike, purport to probe the inner workings of the U.S. Central Intelligence Agency. Many attempt to create spine-tingling suspense or allege that America's civilian spy operation has run amok and been infested with rogues and criminals. Not that *The Craft We Chose* lacks suspense, harrowing encounters, or its own share of villains, but this book is different; it is a straightforward, honest, surprisingly captivating memoir by one of the CIA's most well-known and honored career officers. For more than three decades, Richard L. Holm worked in the agency's Directorate of Operations, now the National Clandestine Service, the component directly responsible for collecting human intelligence. His assignments took him to seven countries on three continents, and his travels added many more destinations. At almost every turn Holm encountered his share of dangerous characters and situations, including one that nearly ended his life before he turned 30. *The Craft We Chose* is more than a chronicle of those episodes. It also reveals Holm's private life, his roots and family, his courtship and marriage, and his four daughters, whom he affectionately calls his platoon.

Praise for *The Craft We Chose*

"A rare and masterful glimpse into the inner workings of the clandestine service ... But more than that, his story is an account of extraordinary personal courage that sets a standard for those who would call themselves intelligence officers."
—**Porter Goss, former Director of Central Intelligence**

"Arguably the best book I have ever read on the agency ... and I've read practically all of them."
—**Larry Cosgriff,** *Maritime Lens*

"Blunt and colorful!"
—**Katharine Whittemore,** *The Boston Globe*

"The stuff of great spy fiction ... a must-read."
—**David Pitt,** *Booklist Online*

"The memoir of a true patriot ... a fascinating look into the motivations and everyday life of a highly decorated CIA operative ... who gave his life--almost literally--to serve our country in ambiguous and dangerous circumstances that we everyday people cannot truly appreciate."
—**Gregory Herbert**

"Remarkable! Thank you for all the work Mountain Lake Press did in bringing this inspiring CIA Officer's autobiography into print in the manner it long deserved."
—**Elizabeth Bancroft, Executive Director, Association of Former Intelligence Officers**

"Clear and engaging ... Holm corrects the media's portrayal of spying operations as car chases punctuated by martinis shaken-not-stirred and disregard for American laws and values."
—**André Le Gallo, former senior CIA officer and author of** *Satan's Spy,* *The Caliphate* **and** *The Red Cell*

"A terrific book–required reading! His story magnifies the importance of human intelligence in warfare, and is demonstrable of the valor of our clandestine services."
—**Frank Gaffney, Secure Freedom Radio**

"Something worth being grateful for--both the book itself and the actual decades of service detailed in its pages."
—**Ronnie Rittenberry,** *Security Products* **magazine**

"A terrific blend of detailed memory, emotional involvement, and fascinating subject matter. Richard Holm put me on his shoulder and walked me through his life, through a variety of cultures in Asia and Europe, and through the twisting corridors of the CIA."
—**Nelson Antonio Denis**

"Well worth reading, not just for the details of the CIA's inner workings but as a chronicle of how one American dealt with adversity to continue serving in the line of work he had, indeed, chosen."
—**Cmdr. Peter B. Mersky, USN (Ret.),** *U.S. Naval Institute Proceedings*

"Thanks for allowing Dick Holm to tell his powerful story of clandestine service to our country. It humbles me to know we have men and women like him and his colleagues keeping us safe at night."
—**Doc Kirby, WTBF-AM/FM, Troy, Alabama**

"An absorbing trip through the mind of a gifted operative who for 35 years did his difficult and sometimes dangerous job to heroic effect ... America was lucky to have him."
—**Charles McCarry,** *The Wall Street Journal*

Decanted Truths

The epic saga of an Irish-American family.

For Irish immigrant families like the Harrigans and Gavagans, struggle has been the name of the game since they arrived in Boston in the nineteenth century. For twice-orphaned Leah Gavagan, who comes of age in the Depression, the struggle is compounded by bizarre visions that disrupt her daily life -- and sometimes come true. She has difficulty fitting in with her surroundings: whether the lace-curtain Dorchester apartment overseen by her judgmental Aunt Margaret or the wild Manomet bluff shared with her no-nonsense Aunt Theo and brain-damaged Uncle Liam. A death in the family disrupts the tepid life path chosen for Leah and sets her on a journey of discovery. That journey goes back to the misadventures shaping the earlier generation, eager to prove its hard-won American credentials in the Alaskan gold rush, the Spanish-American War, and the Great War. She learns of the secrets that have bound Theo and Margaret together. Ultimately, Leah learns she is not who she thought she was. Her new truth both blinds and dazzles her, much like the Waterford decanter at the center of her oldest dreams – an artifact linking three Irish-American families stumbling after the American Dream.

Praise for *Decanted Truths*

"With its pitch-perfect evocation of people and places from a bygone era and interesting premise, the novel is a must read for fans of historical fiction ... A stunning book that expertly explores the difference between mistakes and sins."
 —The Prairies Book Review

"The author did a wonderful job with character development ... *Decanted Truths* is perfect for anyone who wants to get invested in a novel full of secrets... A wonderful book to ... get sucked into."
—The Book Adventures of Emily, book blogger

"This is a great read ... if you like historical stories ... The slight paranormal gifts that you see with the family ... really make the story even more connected."
—Jessica Bronder, JBronder Book Reviews

"Amazing study of two Irish families as they assimilate into America... The author creates a literary novel of intelligence... It is a unique gift, an unusual examination of people."
—Virginia Williams, Rosepoint Publishing

The Hillwilla trilogy

The captivating chronicle of the residents of fictional Seneca County, West Virginia.

 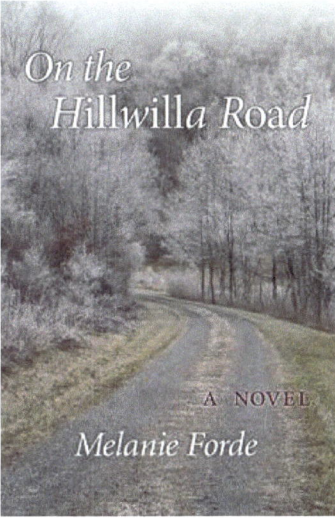 

Beatrice Desmond, 55, lives on a remote farm nestled in a deep hollow in southern West Virginia. Her troubled past—an alcoholic father, growing up borderline poor, a suicidal husband—along with her loyalty to a deceased friend, drove her to this lonely existence. She soldiers on, accompanied by her wry sense of humor, a faithful setter named Ralph, and an inherited herd of six llamas, one of whom hurls a wad of chewed-up hay in her face on New Year's Day, a most unwelcome omen. A native of Boston and a graduate of an Ivy League college, Beatrice is a fish out of water in Seneca County. She has constant difficulty dealing with the wary locals. And although she maintains contact with certain friends and family—lively and irreverent Evie, sturdy brother Bart—they remain distant geographically and sometimes emotionally. As a result, and too often, Beatrice retreats into her work as a translator and editor, or into the bottle of Jack Daniel's she maintains nearby. Fate finally intervenes, requiring Beatrice to befriend and shelter Clara, an abused teenager, and accept the job of ghostwriting the memoir of her dashing but enigmatic neighbor, Tanner Fordyce, the man who bestows the endearment "Hillwilla" on her—the feminine equivalent of the pejorative "Hillbilly." Despite the difficulties, Beatrice eventually finds the harsh Appalachian winter of her life easing and signs of a hopeful spring appearing. Her resolute independence and crusty reserve soften, her carefully constructed barriers fall, and her guarded and self-protective nature moderates, as she explores the renewed pleasures of emotional involvement. At times sad, at times hilarious, and always quirky, *Hillwilla* is a life-affirming read. It celebrates the glories of nature, the resilience of the human spirit, the healing power derived from genuine connections with others, and the potential for reinventing ourselves—at any age.

Praise for *Hillwilla*

"Melanie Forde has given us a 21st-century Back-to-the-Land novel with a troubled protagonist, but also with a preternaturally responsible English setter, an assurance that the ending will be a happy one."
—**Sue Hubbell,** *A Country Year*

"A great, heartwarming story! I loved the scenes; I could feel myself right there in the pages. You can't help getting sucked into the story and keep reading into the late hours wanting to know what is going to happen next. This is a standalone book but I could see other adventures for [Beatrice] in the future. I can't wait to read what Melanie Forde comes up with next."
—**Jessica Bronder, JBronder Book Reviews**

"Forde's writing is insightful, funny, and thought-provoking from start to finish. [Her] poetic delivery of life's spit, sprinkled with the virtues of tolerance, empathy, and humor ... delighted me and gave me pause to reflect. I am not talking sappy, just good writing; writing that connects the reader with the human spirit."
—**Charlie Hackbarth, author,** *Tales of the Trail*

"*Hillwilla* beautifully shows that animals are amazingly human in their love for those they value."
—**Ronald Hart, syndicated libertarian humorist**

"I had a blast in 'Seneca County,' West-by-God Virginia. These characters read as real."
—**Dear Author, book blogger**

"A beautifully written book with a no-nonsense protagonist ... The story is so well crafted, and Melanie has taken a lot of care in introducing and then building up each and every one of her characters."
—**The Bookworm Mummy, book blogger**

On the Hillwilla Road explores how disparate characters can grow to need and depend on one another.

In *Hillwilla*, Beatrice Desmond, a former Bostonian Ivy Leaguer, found herself in midlife on a llama farm in remote West Virginia. Clara Buckhalter, a troubled young girl, drew Beatrice out of her lonely existence. In Melanie Forde's sequel, Clara attends a different school at Beatrice's urging, and finds herself involved with two new friends who are confusing and intimidating yet caring. Beatrice's tantalizing friendship and romance with the dashing, wealthy, and extremely handsome Tanner Fordyce discover new and deeper connections—though they continue to spar and infuriate each other. And Beatrice's farm—replete with temperamental llamas; Ralph, her loyal English setter; and the occasional wild critter—further serves as an oasis of refuge and healing. This sequel explores how such disparate individuals can grow to need and depend on one another, even as Beatrice finds herself confronted with a new, life-altering choice.

Praise for *On the Hillwilla Road*

"A great story and follow up to *Hillwilla*! I couldn't wait to read *On the Hillwilla Road*. Beatrice is still considered an outsider and is trying to find common ground without offending the locals. Clara is trying to find her way and is still so confused. But she is a great kid and you can't help but encourage her. I really like how Beatrice and Tanner are getting closer; I just wanted to slap both of them at times for being so dense and difficult."
—**Jessica Bronder, JBronder Book Reviews**

"This appealing story ... is replete with vivid descriptive passages. "The drama is related from many views, creating a rich tapestry incorporating setting, events and characters ... *On the Hillwilla Road* is a refreshing and thought-provoking book."
—**My Merri Way, book blogger**

In *Reinventing Hillwilla*, Beatrice Desmond's life on the remote llama farm in "Seneca County transitions from contented to chaotic.

The final novel in the *Hillwilla* trilogy unfolds under the watchful eye of canine guardian Ralph. Five years after we first met northern urban transplant Beatrice Desmond, she is finally adapting to her mountain hollow among the wary "born-heres" and is more open to the blessings in her life. She has developed a rewarding mother-daughter relationship with troubled local teenager Clara Buckhalter and is inching toward marriage with dashing, but complicated entrepreneur Tanner Fordyce. Meanwhile, Clara sets off on a productive new path, one that would have been unthinkable had Beatrice never come into her life. All of that progress is suddenly jeopardized by Clara's scheming mother Charyce. Ultimately, the upheaval touched off by Charyce's schemes serves as the catalyst for new beginnings for the Seneca County misfits (even Ralph).

Praise for Reinventing Hillwilla

"The well-paced, well-plotted story creates that bond with characters struggling through discordance with others, loneliness, catastrophic illness, coming of age, long-distance romance and the struggles of survival in harsh, bitter winter conditions ... The author has an intelligent, articulate writing style that pops with little glimmers of Irish humor..."
—**Virginia Williams, Rosepoint Publishing**

"A moving exploration of relationships, family dynamics and notions of home ... Forde draws carefully sketched, rich characters and weaves a convincing reality from their intricate emotions."
—**The Prairies Book Review**

"This story wraps up the series beautifully... with a powerful message about living your life, whether the first half or second ... This is one series that should be on everyone's shelves."
—**Jessica Bronder, JBronder Book Reviews**

Hunting Nukes

A supremely detailed account of a dedicated intelligence officer's half-century effort to fight the apocalyptic threat of proliferation of nuclear weapons, and featuring a Foreword by Ambassador John Bolton.

For fifteen years, Richard Phillip Lawless served as a clandestine-services officer for the Central Intelligence Agency. His primary duty involved seeking out and exposing undeclared nuclear weapons activities within countries of the highest concern to the U.S. government. *Hunting Nukes* is his detailed chronicle of those experiences. Among them, Lawless reveals the successful takedown of the South Korean strategic weapons program in the mid-1970s. He describes, in detail, the Agency's operation that detected, penetrated, defined and eventually blocked that country's covert effort. Reentering U.S. government service in the wake of 9/11, he joined the senior levels of policy-making at the Department of Defense. Lawless recounts his duties as Deputy Undersecretary of Defense for Asian and Pacific Security Affairs, particularly in the 2002-2008 talks with the rogue North Korean regime—the so-called "Six-Party Talks." In those cases and others, Lawless details his role in the political and bureaucratic struggles necessary to keep the world's most terrifying weapons out of the hands of the world's least responsible and most dangerous regimes.

In the Stars

A fascinating collection of essays and reports on astronomy, astrophysics and the planetary sciences at the beginning of the Second Space Age.

In his 40 years as a journalist, the author became well known for his coverage of highway safety and popular culture—particularly the movies. But Phil Berardelli also spent 15 years during that period as a science writer with a special devotion to astronomy and to planetary expeditions. Here, he has collected 60 of his best articles and essays on those topics in a compendium for your background, education and, perhaps, enthusiasm and wonder.

Inside Jihad

An exceptional, vitally needed work that addresses one of the most pressing and dangerous issues of our time.

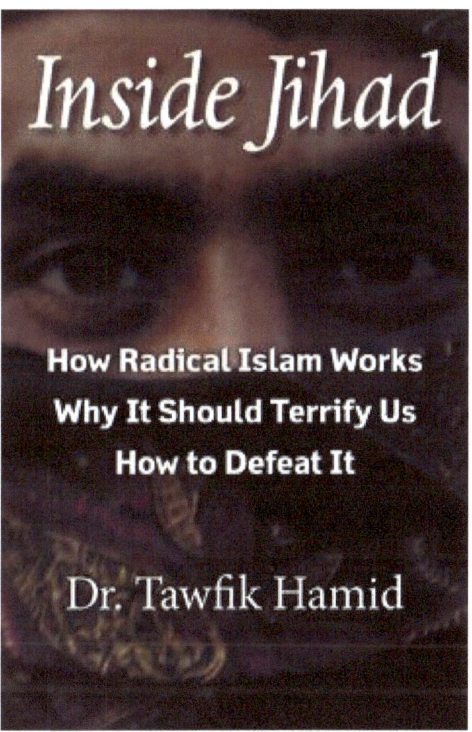

Why has radical Islam become such a deadly threat and why it is so pervasive in the Muslim world? Four decades ago, Tawfik Hamid, then a young medical student, was recruited by Jamaa Islamiyah, an Islamic terror group led by Dr. Ayman al-Zawahiri, the man who replaced Osama bin Laden to become the leader of al-Qaeda. Eventually and miraculously, Hamid recognized the insidious nature of violent *jihad* and rejected its distortions of the Qur'an, the holy book of the Muslim faith. Ever since, he has pursued a path of reformation within Islam by writing new interpretations of the book's key texts and by sharing his message in mosques. ***Inside Jihad*** reveals Dr. Hamid's insights about the Islamic terror movement drawn from his personal experiences. Now a medical doctor and a psychologist, he helps readers understand the jihadist mindset. He also explains the meaning of *jihad* and the role that sex, petrodollars and the *hijab* for women play in its proliferation. And in ***Inside Jihad***, he details his bold plan to reform Islam to end jihadism and its global reign of terror.

Extraordinary praise for Dr. Hamid and *Inside Jihad*

"Reformers such as Tawfik Hamid ... must be supported and protected. They should be as well-known as Solzhenitsyn, Sakharov and Havel were in the 1980s."
—**Ayaan Hirsi Ali**

"*Inside Jihad* is terrific! I wish I had read it 15 years ago when we were trying to decipher radical Islam. I would have made it required reading for my Intel colleagues. It is concise, convincing, compelling—and chilling. I also value *Inside Jihad* so much that I am constantly rereading it. It has become a staple resource kept handy, and I will refer to it regularly in my consulting and speaking events. It is authoritative, definitive and wonderfully politically incorrect."
—**Porter Goss, former Director of Central Intelligence**

"Dr. Tawfik Hamid's knowledge about radical Islam is crucial to understanding and defeating it."
 —**Ambassador R. James Woolsey, former Director of Central Intelligence**

"*Inside Jihad* is an important resource for anyone interested in learning about the thought processes of the jihadists. It will provoke needed discussions as it lays out the fundamental differences between the sects and basic tenets of Islam – vital information in this age of Islamic terrorism."
—**William Esposito, former Deputy Director of the FBI**

"A fascinating look at the driving forces behind radical Islam that provides new insight on how to confront its growing threat around the world today."
—**Senator John McCain**

"This is a riveting and informative work. Dr. Hamid's understanding of how psychological indoctrination creates a radical Islamist is exceedingly useful. He clearly spells out his own indoctrination and focuses on what might undo just such indoctrination."
—**Dr. Phyllis Chesler, Emerita Professor of Psychology, author of 15 books, including *The New Anti-Semitism* and *An American Bride in Kabul***

"*Inside Jihad* is a must-read!"
—**Dr. Zudhi Jasser, founder and president, American Islamic Forum for Democracy and author of *A Battle for the Soul of Islam: An American Muslim Patriot's Fight to Save His Faith***

"A well-written and highly practical guide to understanding and countering radical Islam. It not only defines the threat posed to free society but also contains a compelling, firsthand view of the radicalization process. Dr. Hamid's unique background bolsters the credibility of his insight into the problem and his strategy for a solution."
—**Glen Roberts, Editor, TheReligionofPeace.com**

"[*Inside Jihad*] is a welcome and honest take on the Islamist menace afflicting the world today."
—**Robert Spencer, director of Jihad Watch and best-selling author of 15 books on Islam**

"Without hesitation, I recommend this book to anyone who wants to understand the mind and motives of the jihadist terrorist. Dr. Hamid has done a great service to all persons interested in protecting civilization from barbarism."
—**U.S. Representative Jeff Fortenberry**

"Dr. Hamid's book ought to be read by anyone interested in fighting terrorism. It is timely and insightful."
—**Former U.S. Representative Frank R. Wolf**

"[Tawfik] Hamid is a great scholar whose knowledge of terrorism is extremely valuable. There is no doubt about his first-hand experience and depth of knowledge. He is truly a treasure."
—**Lt. Gen. Claude M. "Mick" Kicklighter, U.S. Army (retired)**

"Everyone in the world affected by the threat of radical Islam needs to read Dr. Hamid's book *Inside Jihad* to understand the dynamics of this dangerous ideology."
—**Maj. Gen. Paul E. Vallely, U.S. Army (retired)**

"Anyone concerned about the proliferation of radical Islam must read this amazing book. *Inside Jihad* not only provides a genuinely comprehensive and historical understanding of how the West has allowed radical Islam to flourish, but more important it also outlines how to defeat it. Dr. Hamid should know better than anyone else. A former member of an Egyptian Islamic terrorist group that eventually merged with al-Qaeda, he made an extraordinarily courageous and unprecedented decision to denounce the terrorist organization once he saw the reality of the horrors of *jihad*. Long before 9/11, he became one of the world's experts on the true dangers of radical Islam. Dr. Hamid has made it his life's mission to reform Islam by

trying to deprogram jihadists from their world of hate and death. He understands Islam in ways that will mesmerize you. Don't wait. Read this book now."
—**Steven Emerson, Executive Director, The Investigative Project on Terrorism**

"*Inside Jihad* is a vital contribution. Anyone who cherishes freedom, faith and family will benefit from engaging its pages ... I urge all concerned with how to overcome the threat of radical Islam to give [it] a well-deserved read."
—**Thomas P. McDevitt, Chairman, *The Washington Times***

"Dr. Tawfik Hamid's book is most timely for [anyone] awakening to the violence and terrorism perpetrated by Islamists *since* 9/11; to read and come to grips with the jihadist mentality. As we should have learned by now, counterterrorism efforts by law-enforcement agencies and the military have their limits. Worse, a full-scale war against Islam and Muslims is exactly what al-Qaeda and ISIS and their ilk want, a war that turns civilizational between the West and Islam, fulfilling the apocalyptic, end-of-the-world scenario they embrace. What urgently needs to be understood is the theological underpinning of Islamism so it can be discredited as a perversion of Islam. Dr. Hamid has performed a great service by deconstructing this theology and showing how Islamists have selectively twisted the meaning of the Quran to justify their hatred of infidels – Jews, Christians, Hindus, Buddhists, non-believers and agnostics – as well as Muslims who reject their jihadism. He has shown how the Islamist quest for a Sharia-based society is driven by the psychology of nihilism and a violent rejection of the modern world. Containing and effectively nullifying Islamist theology will be this century's greatest challenge, for Muslims and non-Muslims alike, and *Inside Jihad* can fortify anyone who commits to this daunting task."
—**Dr. Salim Mansur, Associate Professor of Political Science, University of Western Ontario**

"It is not easy to speak the truth. I have paid a high price for doing so, but I have never felt alone. Dr. Tawfik Hamid is one of the few who has inspired me since I started. He stands as solid as an oak tree, to face an ugly ideology that has destroyed its followers and is destroying the whole world today. Dr. Hamid is a brave and an honest man whom I feel honored and privileged to befriend. I salute and wish him the best!"
—**Dr. Wafa Sultan, author of *A God Who Hates***

"Dr. Tawfik Hamid has a compelling personal story. He's had a front-row seat to radical Islam and has firsthand knowledge of the dangers posed by the growing global *jihad* movement. His is a voice that must be heard."
—**Van D. Hipp, Jr., Chairman, American Defense International, Inc.**

"Mandatory reading for everyone who wants to understand the reality of the threats the world faces. You must know your enemy to defeat your enemy, and Dr. Hamid knows the enemy as only a former jihadist could know."
—**David G. Major, retired FBI executive, founder of the Centre for Counterintelligence and Security Studies**

"Dr. Hamid ... has stood up fearlessly to the tsunami of Islamic extremism to share his tolerant vision of the immediate need for Islam's reformation – to truly become a religion of peace. He has risked himself and his family to fanatic, horrific violence for this "crime." If there is to be hope for a beginning to a better world, and for future generations to be spared endless religious war with massive casualties, then Dr. Hamid is the answer – the personification, the embodiment – of that hope. Should we ignore him, and others like him , and not support their message to the fullest extent, then we shall reap the whirlwind. I am eminently proud, and greatly honored, to call this man my friend. I am grateful to, and blessed by, the Good Lord to think of him as my brother."
—**Dr. Robert Katz, Executive Director, The Intelligence Summit ᴤᴹ**

"Dr. Tawfik Hamid understands the jihadist mind because it was once his mind. He knows the way in and the way out. This makes his analysis indispensable in terms of its depth of spiritual insight. Anyone interested in countering this demented religious ideology should read this book."
—**Robert R. Reilly, author of *The Closing of the Muslim Mind***

"*Inside Jihad* is a must-read for anyone seeking to better understand radical Islam, the reasons why this malignancy has found a fertile environment within the Muslim world, and the failures of the West in crafting an effective counter-narrative."
—**Dr. Paul Coyer, International Institute of Strategic Studies and The Institute of World Politics, writing in Providence magazine.**

"A very important book that draws on [Dr. Hamid's] experiences with *jihad* in his native Egypt."
—**Frank Gaffney, Secure Freedom Radio**

Mr. Bridges

The heartbreaking but engrossing second novel from a writer with rare literary gifts.

Jack Bridges is the popular principal at Great Forest elementary school in suburban Washington, D.C. His easy manner and likeability contribute to his success and job satisfaction. Each day, he attends to his work and then returns home to his wife Greta and their three young sons, Chris, Bud, and Sam. Nina Talbott is a housewife living near the elementary school. She is raising her two daughters, Polly and Elaine, while her husband Tom travels frequently to meet the needs of his job. Eventually, and inevitably, Jack and Nina become attracted to each other and consummate a passionate affair, thereby setting into motion a relationship full of excitement but fraught with guilt and regrets. Jack also experiences a personal epiphany when he returns to the small Michigan lakeside town where he spent an idyllic youth. The experience, followed by a personal tragedy, forces Jack to make a fateful and likely irrevocable life choice. Set in the 1980s, Jessie Thorpe's enthralling second novel contains the signature intelligence and piercing insights into the human condition she displayed in **Bolton Roper**, her highly praised debut work. She infuses every page with irresistible details and lush descriptions. She has rapidly established herself as one of literary fiction's premier writers, an author whose work, as one respected critic has described, is extraordinary.

Praise for *Mr. Bridges*

"Unreservedly recommended"

"Following author Jessie Thorpe's acclaimed debut novel **Bolton Roper**, her new title, **Mr. Bridges**, is deftly set in the 1980s and once again showcases her natural flair as a novelist for both originality and the kind of narrative-driven storytelling style replete with the types of details and descriptions that provide a feeling of authenticity, believability, and reader engagement that raise a novel to the level of fine literature."
—Midwest Book Review

"A true literary novel"

"Jessie Thorpe puts the 'literary' in literary novels. Her latest, **Mr. Bridges**, is filled with textural shadings. There are lush descriptions of natural settings. There are also tight dialogue snippets that convey character and relationships with remarkable economy of language. 'Literary' doesn't mean inaccessible in this simple story, driven by flawed but engaging characters who aren't all that dissimilar from the guy down the street. There aren't many books that keep me reading until 3:00 a.m. **Mr. Bridges** did.
—Melanie Forde

Phil's three Favorite 500s

A trio of informative, consistently entertaining guides to classic movies.

 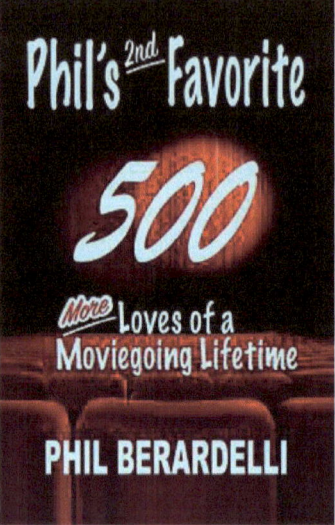 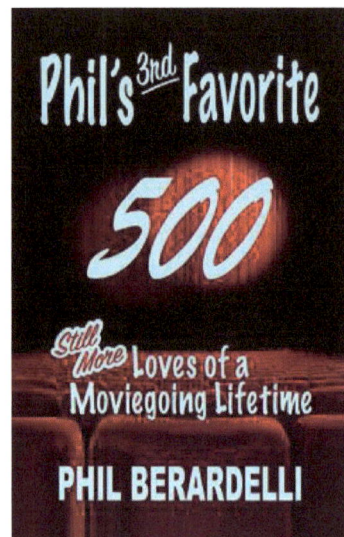

Phil Berardelli has been in love with movies ever since his first encounter as a little boy thrilled him and then scared the daylights out of him. In the intervening years, including a six-year stint as a TV movie critic, Phil has seen at least 5,000 titles. Here he has put together a list of his 500+ favorites, which he has separated into 50 categories. He has accompanied each one with informative, witty, and often insightful capsule comments along with bits of trivia, formatting descriptions and, where available, links to online trailers, clips and full-length versions. *Phil's Favorite 500* encompasses everything Phil has learned in over half a century of moviegoing. The list includes something for everyone – adults, couples, children, teens and families – and covers some of the greatest movies ever made, both in the U.S. and elsewhere, as well as some of the cinema's most entertaining clunkers. Many of his choices – and omissions – might surprise you. But in all cases, Phil makes compelling arguments for sampling these titles. If you do browse the selections, you might just find yourself adding many of them to your own list of favorites. Whether sampled, browsed or read from beginning to end, *Phil's Favorite 500* reflects a love of the medium that is contagious, and his descriptions will help you view even the most familiar movies in a new and very entertaining way.

In *Phil's 2nd Favorite 500*, don't be misled by the name. The new list contains many, many movies that are well worth seeing and full of memorable moments. He encourages you to consider his suggestions and see if you agree that the world of cinema contains a vast bounty of enjoyment for moviegoers of all ages and tastes. As in *Phil's Favorite 500*, the second compilation contains, along with sparkling commentary, bits of interesting trivia, some of it unique to Phil's own experiences as a movie critic. He invites you to discover for yourself the many pleasures of his 2nd Favorite 500.

And in *Phil's 3rd Favorite 500*, he adds yet another 500 titles, presented in yet another 50 categories. With this trilogy, Phil offers a vast array of attractions to engage a wide variety of interests, from the most avid film students to the most casual viewers, and ranging from acknowledged classics to little-known treasures. All represent some of the finest work of moviemakers in America and overseas alike, with some titles going back nearly a hundred years. Witty and eminently browsable, Phil's three compilations will no doubt in the coming years be regarded as classic references for movie lovers everywhere.

Praise for *Phil's Favorite 500*

"**Descriptively informative.**"

"Thoroughly 'film fan friendly' in organization and presentation – making it an essential and welcome addition to personal, professional, community, film school, college and university library Cinematic History reference collections and supplemental curriculum studies lists."
—**Midwest Book Review**

"One of the most lavishly expansive and browsable books ever published."
—**Gary Arnold, former film critic of The Washington Post and The Washington Times**

"**The essential movie guide!**"

"Not only is the book incredibly informative about every important or original film, it is witty and a pleasure to read. And unlike most modern film guides, it distills the history of great movie-making down to the 500 most significant films, movies that anyone who loves movies must see."
—**Robert Zimmerman, host of BehindtheBlack.com**

The Quarryman's Girl

Melanie Forde's fifth novel is a tour-de-force portrait of a former Quebecoise woman's life and family in early 20th century Quincy, Massachusetts.

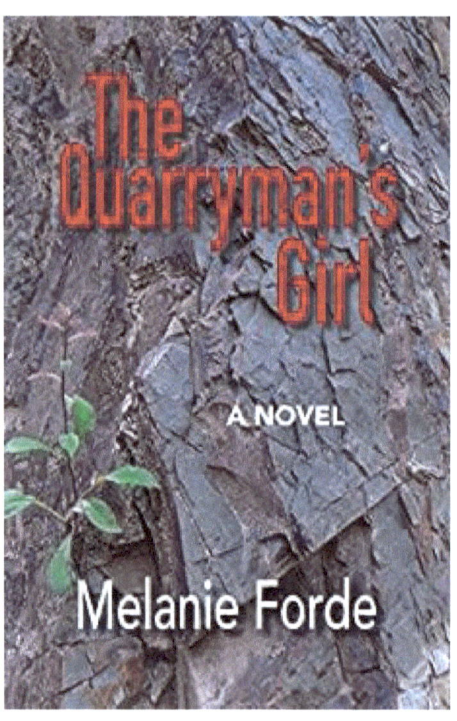

Life seemed to be winding down for French–Canadian immigrant Rose Dowd. She had not been fighting the inevitable until Fate forced her to gear up for yet another chapter. Much like her adopted country, as America begins staking out a new international role in World War II, Rose must reinvent herself. Quickly. Before she can move forward, however, she needs to absorb the lessons from her past. Integral to that journey are Rose's sharp-tongued sister Izzy; her perpetually worried son Vince, a resourceful shipyard worker; her long-dead Métis mentor Mère Agathe; her bright and bubbly but sickly granddaughter Netty; and Nate, the "Ragman's Grandson," a club-footed, pre-law student dreading his future and inching instead toward a career as a writer. The Quarryman's Girl follows these vivid characters from the 1880s to the 1940s, from the hard-scrabble pig farms of Quebec to the granite quarries of Quincy, from the frozen St. Lawrence to the deep-channel Fore River. A compelling story from beginning to end, once again Melanie Forde has shown why she is a consummate storyteller and one of contemporary America's finest novelists.

Praise for *The Quarryman's Girl*

"This beautifully penned literary novel is deeply entwined with characters so well developed you want to hug them. They're family!"
—**Virginia Williams, Rosepoint Publishing**

"A captivating piece of historical fiction. Forde merges human drama and historical intrigue in her compelling latest novel. She structures the plot with plenty of satisfying twists, and she gives her characters complexity, rendered in well-crafted prose. Although the narrative touches on complex topics, such as familial ties, trust, betrayal, aspirations and failures, most of the story focuses on the intense relationships among people trying to make sense of a world turned upside down. Human connection, especially, is at the center of the book. The pacing is measured, the storyline is intriguing, and Forde avoids the familiar melodrama and sentimentality to which a lesser writer might succumb. A gem of a novel."
—**The Prairies Book Review**

"A wonderfully crafted novel with deeply explored and sophisticated characters. The author excels at writing family dynamics, allowing the relationships between the heroine and loved ones to shine through the narrative ... [Forde] enriches the writing by deftly developing themes of family dynamics, betrayal, and loyalty, and by infusing the writing with humanity and realism."
—**Romuald Dzemo**, The Book Commentary

"Readers are transported into a world of heartrending family dynamics, the power of forgiveness, and the struggles of aging ... The story is poignant, exploring the emotional complexities of familial and friendly bonds, encompassing love, injury, and physical and mental limitations of its characters while portraying senior cognitive degeneration honestly. The scenes are meticulously drawn and border on the cinematic, bringing to life the landscape with prose like, 'Random shafts of sunlight penetrated the depths and allowed a distorted view of the massive rock walls all around.' The book is rich in emotion, with raw and humorous moments that alternate. The writing style is perceptive, sophisticated, and eloquent with a closing that is certain to elicit a deeply moving response. Very highly recommended.
—**Asher Syed, Readers' Favorite Reviews**

The Safe Driving Trilogy

An invaluable set of guides to improve safety on the road at any age or level of experience.

Safe Young Drivers has been called the best book on driving instruction ever written. Now in its 26th year in print, Phil Berardelli's guide has helped tens of thousands of families launch their teens with care and wisdom. The process began in 1996, after Phil had published articles on safe-driving techniques in several major newspapers, and after repeated requests from parent groups for reliable advice on teaching teens to drive. An instant critical and commercial success, Phil has nevertheless periodically updated and refined the book's content. *Safe Young Drivers* is an invaluable resource for surviving the most dangerous environment we all face every day.

Praise for *Safe Young Drivers*

"One of the best investments you'll make in your child's life ... This is a book that every parent trying to teach a teenager to drive should read."
—**Judy Mann, The Washington Post**

"This is an invaluable book you absolutely must read before you allow your teenager behind the wheel of a car."
—**Dr. Laura Schlessinger**

"*Safe Young Drivers* is a recommended resource for any parent; I'll use it in teaching my own teens."
—**Kevin Wilson, Executive Editor, *AutoWeek***

"**Safe Young Drivers** is ... filled with facts and advice about everything you'd want your child to know about safe driving."
—**GEICO Today**

"This book takes a great approach ... with a lot of good tips and some great ideas."
—**Jack Ford, NBC, The Today Show**

"*Safe Young Drivers* ... is a book that deals with these parental problems and the teen driver VERY effectively."
"**Mr. Traffic," syndicated radio host**

"I suggest that parents or family members provide driver education and ... I recommend starting with the book Safe Young Drivers."
—**Ron Shaffer, "Dr. Gridlock," *The Washington Post***

"The book is a gem."
Susan Richman, Pennsylvania Homeschoolers

The Driving Challenge: a blunt but invaluable tool for improving your driving skills – at any age

During 2020, when millions and millions of people obsessed – sometimes to the point of outright panic – over a contagious virus called COVID, a different plague, which had been gradually receding, began re-emerging with a vengeance. It turned out that 2020 was also a landmark year for deaths and injuries from highway collisions. Both rose by stunning amounts over the previous year. Overall, the jump in highway deaths per miles traveled spiked by 24 percent, the worst such figure in the entire century-long history of such statistics. Why did this happen? It seems that as traffic diminished because of the country's limits on travel and business and social gatherings, those who remained on the roads exhibited unrestrained boldness, with tragic but predictable results. In the 20 years since Phil Berardelli first published *The Driving Challenge*, experience has shown his safe-driving techniques to be reliable and easy to follow. Now, with the carnage on our highways again spiraling upward, drivers need Phil's advice perhaps more than ever. So, make a small investment in your safety -- take *The Driving Challenge*!

And with *Drive On!* six experienced writers take on perhaps the most challenging highway safety issue of all: how seniors can continue driving while prudently and continually assessing their skills on the road

Are you a Baby Boomer? A member of the post-World War II generation? Retiring or planning to retire at a time when U.S. life expectancy has never been higher? If so, you re part of the exploding population of senior drivers on our highways. You re also helping to create potentially massive problems for traffic planners, highway safety engineers and healthcare providers who are struggling to cope with the challenge of tens of millions of aging Americans plying the roadways... Or are you? In *Drive On!*, six talented writers most of them senior drivers themselves have tackled this question head-on. They've sorted through the many myths and misperceptions about senior drivers. They've consulted the best available research. And they've drawn on their own collective decades of experience to reach a surprising and welcome conclusion: You can stay safe behind the wheel for many years if you follow their advice and learn from their insights. You will also enjoy their fascinating interviews, easy-to-use self-diagnostic quizzes and compelling personal stories, all packaged within this unique, concise and most entertaining little book. If you're a senior driver, or about to become one, *Drive On!* is invaluable!

The Safehaven Chronicles

Three brief but unforgettable novels about a doctor's tragic but redemptive life.

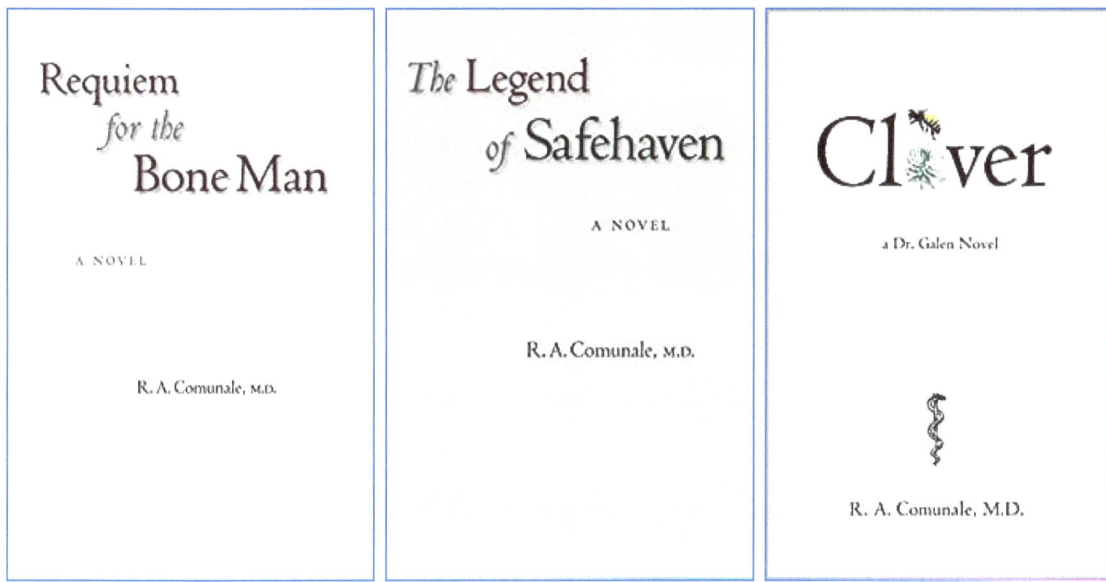

Requiem for the Bone Man is a moving, compelling first novel, told with the assurance and skill of a born storyteller. It is also a meditation on the art of healing, as seen in the adventures of its unforgettable central character, Dr. Robert Galen. From his youth as a street-smart son of immigrants to his career as a gifted physician, Galen is tough-minded yet compassionate. Above all, he is deeply human, willing to risk the pain of loss and failure that inevitably comes to those with an unshakeable commitment to a vocation and to friends and loved ones.

The Legend of Safehaven is the sequel to R. A. Comunale's highly praised first novel ***Requiem for the Bone Man***. This story follows Dr. Robert Galen and his friends, Robert and Nancy Edison, as they adjust to semi-retirement on a mountaintop in northeastern Pennsylvania, raising and caring for the three orphaned Hidalgo children they rescued and adopted. Along the way, the six residents of the mountain interact with a variety of individuals human and animal who also are seeking sanctuary, and even redemption, on the property that becomes known as Safehaven. In ways mystical, magical, and even heroic, Comunale once again envelops readers in a fictional world that is often harrowing, but always captivating.

Clover recalls again the childhood of the man who would grow up to become Dr. Robert Galen. His story began with the chance discovery of a dead woman on a dingy river bank in New Jersey changed the life of 8-year-old Robert Galen forever; it propelled him into a lifelong study of medicine, beginning under the sage counsel of his mentor, Dr. Agnelli. In turn, his medical career led him to two ill-fated marriages and one would-be recaptured romance. Then, alone and in near despair, Galen found a new reason for being, in his old friend Bob Edison, along with his patient wife, Nancy, and in the three, orphaned Hidalgo children, whom he rescued from the wrath of a hurricane. Together, the six and a host of other injured souls attained solace living at Safehaven, the often-miraculous refuge perched on the side of a mountain in the endless hills of northeastern Pennsylvania. R.A. Comunale chronicled this deeply human saga in his first two novels, *Requiem for the Bone Man* and *The Legend of Safehaven*, both of which won him widespread praise for his vivid characters and sharp insights into the human condition. Now, in the third installment of the series, Comunale brings the residents of Safehaven together once more, perhaps for the last time.

Readers' praise for the Safehaven Chronicles

"[*Requiem for the Bone Man*] is an excellent read that I could not put down. The character development was superb and the story both fascinating and very compelling. You feel as if you have known the main characters for years ... you both feel their pain and share their joys. I have shared this book with many friends and without exception, all have greatly enjoyed the book as well!"
—**Dan Sweeney**

Fortunately, I didn't have to wait too long [for] *The Legend of Safehaven*, another wonderfully told story. This book takes place in my beloved home state of Pennsylvania, where we watch the three children who were adopted in *Requiem for the Bone Man* by Nancy and Bob Edison grow up and Nancy, Bob and Dr. Galen enter their 'golden years'! We meet interesting new characters who, of course, are welcomed and nurtured at Safehaven by the ever compassionate Dr. Galen and his friends. There are some great surprises in this volume that include a child with Autism and many devoted 'friends' from the animal kingdom. Dr. Comunale paints in words with the same compassion, humor and expertise with which he practices medicine. This is another 'you just can't put it down' - you MUST keep reading!"
—**Betty Ann Yurkewitch**

"The ebb and flow [of *Clover*] was wonderful. The sweetness of new love and love at any age was sweet and from my perspective very relatable. I generally do not read fiction however his series of nooks have been a wonderful experience for me. Recommend it for anyone that likes to 'feel emotions' when reading."
—**Charles W. Purcell**

Save Gas? Drive Safe!

In these days of sky-high motor-fuel prices, here's an eminently practical guide to reducing your costs significantly – beginning with the very next time you get behind the wheel.

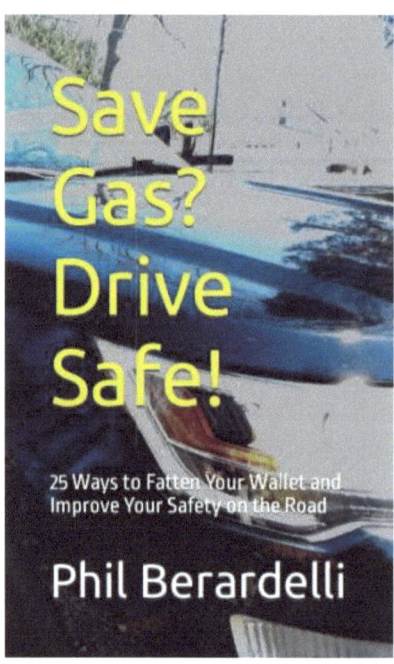

Fed up with sky-high prices for gasoline and diesel fuel? Wondering what in the world you can do about it -- not next year or even next month, but now? Here's a great new book by Phil Berardelli, an acknowledged expert on driving issues, that can help you reduce your motor-fuel bills starting with the next time you head out on the road. All it takes is some common sense and self-discipline. Follow the concise tips Phil lays out in these pages, and you are guaranteed to cut fuel consumption -- and save money. Even better, Phil's tactics are designed to increase the odds that each trip will be safer and more pleasant as well as more thrifty.

Small Wonders

An exquisite sampler, as the subtitle reveals, of reviews and commentary by a most engaging writer.

You might not have heard of Jessie Thorpe or read any of her reviews during 2002 and 2003. But during her time at United Press International, she quickly gained a loyal following for her breezy but insightful critiques of books, films and occasional social events. One newspaper even created a special design for her featured reviews. It was fitting. Using her lifetime love and study of literature and nonfiction, Jessie Thorpe had developed the keenest of eyes for spotting new and emerging talents -- and for poking well-deserved holes into substandard works by famous authors and personalities. Her book reviews consistently presented unique perspectives and insights, and her thoughtful essays matched the observational prowess of much more widely known commentators. They remain trenchant and persuasive despite the passage of time. So, if you love literature, if you appreciate a clear thinker, please sample the small wonders presented here.

The Steve Church Saga

Gripping counterterror novels, written by a former top intelligence officer who experienced, for real, many of the thrilling episodes in this extraordinary trilogy.

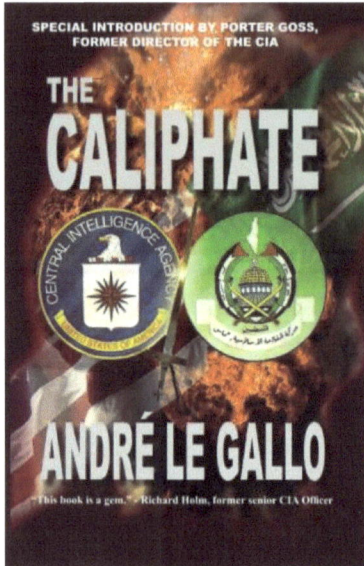  

Written by former master spy and master storyteller André Le Gallo – who passed away in 2017 after a long illness—the trilogy paints a vivid, fictionalized picture of the intense but covert war that has been going on between Iran and the United States since the Tehran hostage crisis of 1979.

In *The Caliphate*, a radical Muslim group has dedicated itself to the restoration of the global Islamic empire based on cruel medieval values and the conquests of the faith's glory years. These true believers will stop at nothing, including assassinations and terrorism, to achieve their goal. Standing in their way is Steve Church, just a U.S. businessman in Paris who never expected to be recruited by the CIA as an undercover operative. But now, with his life on the line, with the fate of nations at stake, and with the safety of his beautiful Kella in jeopardy, Steve must dive headlong into a desperate struggle to prevent mass destruction. *The Caliphate* is a whirlwind adventure, bristling with exotic locales, dangerous and desperate characters, and international intrigue, all crafted by a former master spy who has experienced similar dangers and challenges firsthand.

Praise for *The Caliphate*

"I cannot think of any more crucial topic and anyone more qualified to discuss the Iranian situation than Mr. André Le Gallo, who witnessed the Iranian revolution firsthand and [observed] how the radical Islamists took the government apart. Will Egypt, Algeria, Tunisia and others follow?"
—**Farhad Mansourian, former military intelligence officer, Iranian Army**

Then, in *Satan's Spy*, Islamic terrorists attempt to take over the hotel where Steve Church is staying in Bahrain, forcing him to use his CIA training to blunt the attack. That same day, the Director of the National Clandestine Service calls Steve to tell him he is needed at agency headquarters–urgently. Soon thereafter, Steve and his live-in girlfriend Kella, a former French intelligence officer, are off on a dangerous mission to collect intelligence on Iran's nuclear program. In the process, they learn the Islamic state is also preparing a massive cyberattack against the United States. Like *The Caliphate*, its predecessor, *Satan's Spy* is a whirlwind adventure bristling with exotic locales, dangerous and desperate characters, and international intrigue, all crafted by former master spy Le Gallo, who experienced many of the same dangers and challenges firsthand.

Praise for *Satan's Spy*

"Who can tell a story better than the person in charge of CIA in Tehran at the time of Iranian Islamic Revolution and a high level CIA Operations expert."
—**Farhad Mansourian, former military intelligence officer, Iranian Army**

And in *The Red Cell*, Steve Church and Kella Hastings, members of the titular CIA out-of-the-box unit, find themselves in the crosshairs of the Quds Force, Iran's elite commando group, as payback for a recent operation against the Tehran regime. In a series of thrusts and counter-thrusts, Steve and Kella battle General Ghassem Yosemani, the Quds Force commander, in operations and escapes that take them across Brussels, Paris, New York, and finally San Francisco, as Yosemani becomes ever more determined to kill Steve and Kella and wreak chaos and devastation on the U.S. economy.

Praise for *The Red Cell*

"Few [former intelligence officers] are able to write espionage stories that are realistic, clever, and entertaining. Le Gallo is one of those few and has done it again with *The Red Cell*."
—**The Intelligencer**

"André Le Gallo [has done] it again! [**The Red Cell**] is the third in a trilogy of action-packed, 'round-the-world adventure. The real James Bond would only wish to have Le Gallo's real-life experiences. I know André, and he is the real deal; grace, guts and gallantry—a true American hero!"
—**Dr. Barry Austin Goodfield, International Criminal Profiler**

FEATURED REVIEWS

Adventures in the Scream Trade

Retired operatic baritone Charles Long emerges from the pages of this neatly titled memoir as a person of such colorful vitality as to make me sad that I never encountered him in performance. To make a career as a performer, let it be confessed, needs a degree of self-confidence that unsympathetic observers may see as arrogance. What is interesting about Mr. Long is that this quality coexists with a rarer, and rather touching, awareness of his own weaknesses. The result is a self-portrait of more than average polychromatic richness. Long's well-written story juxtaposes his 'scenes from operatic life,' which provide a revealing account of what might be called the engine-room of opera performance, with a no less interesting confessional of his often bumpy relationships and the health problems that led to his regrettably early retirement after some glorious years sharing the stage, on evidently equal terms, with many of the greatest singers of our time. The book is attractively produced, and offers entertaining reading for anyone interested in music–or, for that matter, in human strengths and foibles.
—**Bernard Jacobson, independent music critic, Seattle, Washington**

Among Enemies

When we examine a piece of intelligence or analysis, it is wise to determine, among other factors, both the bona fides and the access of the source, and Luke Bencie more than passes muster on both scales. The brief *About the Author* section at the end of the book establishes Bencie as having traveled to over 100 countries over the past 15 years on behalf of the U.S. Intelligence Community, as well as for the private defense industry, and as having become aware, sometimes painfully he says, of the extents to which both foreign governments, industrial and even freelance operators will go to steal American business secrets.

Among Enemies is a primer for American business travelers, designed both to inform them of the threats they may face, on the parts of unfriendly parties, to their proprietary information, and to teach them, to some degree, how to think and act like a counterintelligence officer. Bencie identifies the information sought by the adversary as both business intelligence and intellectual property, BI/IP and, while acknowledging the technical differences between them, treats them as a single unit for unfriendly collection.

He properly dwells at some length on the significant and growing threat of cyberattacks on the various electronic devices carried by the business traveler, and what can be done to minimize or deflect these. He recommends a laptop dedicated to business travel which contains only the information germane to the current travel and is professionally scrubbed between travels. Any BI/IP necessary to be with the traveler should be on a thumb drive and neither device should ever be outside the control of the traveler. Tablets and cell phones are equally vulnerable and should be protected with equal care.

Three primary threat areas facing the traveler are the plane, the taxi and the hotel. A seat companion on the plane and the loquacious cabbie could both be professional experts in elicitation and the friendly and gregarious American is all too frequently an easy target. Threats in the hotel have come a long way from the day when what we feared most was the concealed microphone in the room. The audio threat is still there, of course, and is now complemented by the video, frequently above the work area so the camera can read what is being produced on the laptop, and the cyber threat that no physical examination will detect. The author quite properly discourages physical examination of the room in any case first, because what has been professionally concealed will not be found and, more importantly, because such an examination will be noted by the adversary who may well conclude that our traveler has had counterintelligence training and may himself be an intelligence officer. Either of these could be detrimental to the business purpose of the trip and, depending on the country, could lead to host government counterintelligence interest. In either case, the business purpose of the trip will not have been met.

It is not only host government intelligence/security services that will be interested in acquiring BI/IP. An entire industry of private collectors has arisen, frequently staffed by former government professionals, who collect information to sell to the people with whom the traveler is there to meet. They could be commissioned to do this, or they could be acting on their own initiative after having identified our traveler as a potential target of opportunity. These private collectors are aided by the free-lancers, that taxi driver who may have come up with what is effectively an operational lead in the course of an airport to hotel ride, and receives a one-time payment from the professional who then pursues it.

The author correctly notes that attention to all these potential threats need not and should not result in paranoia, but rather in that professional virtue we call situational awareness. Being conscious of the threat even before departing on the travel, being aware from moment to moment while abroad of one's immediate situation, and being willing to acknowledge that, while in the foreign country, one is effectively either always on or not far from that operational X, can lead to avoiding or minimizing unfriendly collection efforts and contribute to the success of the trip. It will not be fun, but it is not a vacation.

—Jack Lee, Vice President, Florida Satellite Chapter, Association of Former Intelligence Officers

Bolton Roper

A deftly crafted novel by an author with a genuine flair for originality and the kind of narrative driven storytelling style that will keep the reader's fully engaged attention from first page to last, **Bolton Roper** is an extraordinary and unreservedly recommended addition to community library General Fiction collections.
—**Midwest Book Review**

The Craft We Chose

Very late in **The Craft We Chose: My Life in the CIA**, author Richard L. Holm writes, "The United States continues to defend itself against enemies who are hell-bent on destroying us. The National Clandestine Service is playing a vital part in that seemingly unending fight because electronic intelligence gathering can take us only so far. The human element is indispensable and must endure." Those lines echoed in my head for days after I set the book aside, and now I think I know why. For one thing, I had just read more than 500 pages recounting circumstances and events that clearly demonstrated the indispensability of one human—Holm—and what a difference he made in what we call history, or even reality.

Holm's memoir—his second, for the record—covers more than three decades, beginning with his joining the CIA's Junior Officer Training program in 1960 and ending with his retirement in 1996, the same year he received the Distinguished Intelligence Medal, the agency's highest award. Those 36 years—more than a lifetime for too many of his fellow agents—spanned the Vietnam War, Watergate and its aftermath, the Iran-Contra affair and the end of the Cold War, among many other chapters of history. During those events—indeed, while enswirled in them and later dealing with their fallout—Holm steadily rose through agency ranks, working in the Directorate of Operations—now the National Clandestine Service, the component directly responsible for collecting human intelligence—and eventually becoming one of the agency's senior operations officers. His career included deployments to seven countries on three continents and service under 13 CIA directors.

The book's chapters, and the years they represent, fly by, with Holm's first-person accounts setting the reader squarely in the midst of them. Throughout, Holm maintains focus on the art and craft of intelligence (and counterintelligence) gathering, consistently referring to it as 'tradecraft' as matter-of-factly as others might discuss shoemaking or metallurgy. He writes:

> *Most movies and the media in general portray agency personnel as either cloak-and-dagger types, sometimes with superhuman abilities, or*

ruthless bureaucrats who would rather sacrifice one of their own than give up power. The fact is we do sometimes train people extensively before we dispatch them on dangerous missions. It's also true that once in a while a rogue wave washes its way into our sea of personnel.

But the overwhelming truth is that most of what we do parallels government work in general and much of the private sector. Some of it is downright ordinary, involving mountains of paperwork. Someone has to supervise that ordinary but important work. For a while, and for a part of it, that someone had to be me.

Before eventually becoming a "headquarters bureaucrat" (his phrase), Holm served the agency as a "man on the street" (also his phrase, although given the crude conditions of some of his missions, it's using the phrase loosely). And, as his publisher contends, Holm's story does contain "suspense worthy of a Hollywood blockbuster or a best-selling novel."

One of the most riveting (and, in retrospect, cinematic) episodes involves Holm's survival, at age 29, of a harrowing plane crash in central Africa's Congo that burned more than 35 percent of his body and led to the loss of his left eye. Holm survived the surreal ordeal on sheer determination ('I simply would not die in this rotten Congo, I decided') and with the angelic assistance of an unnamed Azande witch doctor and a small band of men who walked and rode bicycles 100 miles across enemy-held and cannibal-infested territory to reach help.

Many years later, while serving as a station chief in Europe and as head of a U.S. counterterrorism group, Holm participated in the hunt for the international terrorist and assassin known as Carlos the Jackal. While caught up in the reading of such experiences, it is easy to forget that Holm and his fellow agents were doing such work—and routinely facing danger as part of it—without the benefit of technologies that were anywhere on par with the systems and devices highlighted every month in the pages of this magazine. At the time, such technologies simply didn't exist, but even if they had, Holm's observation about the limitations of electronic intelligence gathering would still ring true.

Holm's memoir is a testament to that fact, and it's a good reminder for those in the security profession at whatever level—local, national or international. As good of a read as it is, though, **The Craft We Chose** is a book that almost didn't happen.

In the memoir's final pages, Holm credits former CIA Director Richard Helms with convincing him to overcome reservations he had about chronicling his mostly secret career. Helms, Holm says, advised keeping in mind a larger purpose.

"If we don't write about the Cold War period it will be written by journalists and academics, and they will get it wrong," Helms said, to which Holm writes, by way of reply, "I couldn't disagree with him. Dick Helms knew it is imperative for Americans to understand and support what the CIA does. To put it plainly, the agency needs a constituency. He believed, and I concur wholeheartedly, that the more the public appreciates what we do, the stronger their support will be."

Even if scholars and media types earnestly attempt the task of reporting the years Holm covers and try to get things right, they will necessarily lack the insider vantage of Holm's lifetime on the streets and behind closed doors. His work is something worth being grateful for—both the book itself and the actual decades of service detailed in its pages.

—**Ronnie Rittenberry, print managing editor for *Security Products* and *Occupational Health and Safety* magazines**

Decanted Truths

Decanted Truths: An Irish-American Novel by Melanie Forde is a multi-decade saga of three Irish families: the Harrigans, the Gavagans, and the Costellos. In a story of secrets, lies, and family values, different characters share their journeys with readers as one particular person takes the brunt of the pressure. Leah Gavagan believes she was cursed. A child of Irish immigrants who settled in Boston for a better future, Leah was an orphan living with her Aunt Theo. Leah had visions she could not explain. She sometimes felt alienated, but she was not the first person in her family to feel that way. As the past revealed itself and we learn more about the previous Harrigans and Gavagans, it became clear that Leah was one piece of a whole picture that slowly unveiled itself.

Interesting and equally fascinating, *Decanted Truths* had many characters, each with a story to tell. Author Melanie Forde divided the story into three parts for good reason. I appreciated how she introduced each character before the story began and guided us to remember who was who. It was daunting but exciting at the same time. It gave us a timeline and let me picture what was happening in the background. Leah was miserable initially, but it changes as the story progressed. Instead of hiding from the world and herself, she dug deep and looked for answers that always evaded her. I felt bad for Margaret, who was looking for comfort but could not find it. Liam, Theo, Ned, and others were searching for something they longed for, while Leah, Philly, and Teddy were looking for answers while figuring out their place among peers. Melanie ensured the story's setting was beautifully described, the characters developed at their own pace, and allowed the story to mature independently. It all connected so well in the end, and the intricacy of the plot blew me away. I highly recommend this novel to anyone who enjoys family sagas with secrets and acceptance.

—**Rabia Tanveer, Readers' Favorite**

Hillwilla

Melanie Forde's hauntingly stark cover photo, along with the book's curious title, makes a powerful first impression. In fact it was enough to induce the "Fargo" willies in me. And I have to say, after reading the first short chapters, "Spit Happens," "Bart Sighs," and "Post-Holiday Blues," that although *Hillwilla* seems a long way from "Fargo," I thought it would turn out to be a melancholy book. Indeed, it might well have if not for Forde's wonderful way with words. The further I read, the more obvious it became that this author has something she's been itching to say. And I love the way she says it

Spit does happen in *Hillwilla*, just as it happens in everyday life. Some of it washes off easily and is forgotten, but some of it stains deep in the heart. If you're looking for something that will give you the Fargo willies, this is not the book for you. If you are looking for a love story, *Hillwilla* certainly has those aspects. But for me it's Melanie Forde's poetic delivery of life's spit, sprinkled with the virtues of tolerance, empathy, and humor, which delighted me and gave me pause to reflect. It's writing that connects the reader with the human spirit.
—**Charlie Hackbarth, author,** *Tales of the Trail*

The Quarryman's Girl

The wait is often worth it.

Such is the case with this beautifully penned literary novel deeply entwined with characters so well developed you want to hug them. They're family.

I was introduced to this author back in 2019 with the request for participation in a book tour; one I was glad to accept for **Reinventing Hillwilla** (final novel in the Hillwilla trilogy) followed a few months later by **Decanted Truths**. I loved them both, each read as a standalone and each entirely unique.

In this novel, Rose Dowd is staring down seniorhood and doesn't like what she sees. Thank heaven she has Vince, her youngest son, to help her meet day-to-day challenges she was formerly capable of handling on her own after her husband passed on. She also has others in her life well established near the granite quarries of Quincy (KWIN-zee—not KWIN-see) where she and estranged sister Izzy were abandoned after her large Irish family left Quebec and Quincy for Manitoba. The girls, barely teens, survived and thrived.

There are a number of threads interweaving through the well-plotted narrative, and we get to know each of the characters, identify easily with people we know, care about, invest in. Descriptions of scenes are so well drawn that the reader is plunked into the middle of them. Loved the inclusion of the French phrases in the storyline as well as the Native American's contribution to the shipyard efforts—the dialogue between Vince and Walter, a Mohawk, is priceless male banter.

Tension builds as the characters are developed and Nate, the "Ragman's Son," is sent to perform handyman jobs at Rose's home and to report to Vince her slips of memory. Nate is frustrated with Rose's senior moments as he tries in vain to glean grist for a thesis, unhappily facing law school.

And then there is Izzy, her sharp tongue alienating more than immediate family, who has a crisis of her own that may force Rose to deal with the upheaval that caused their rift so many years ago.

Oh, so bittersweet, examining the hurts, the love, the physical as well as the mental constraints that bind family and friends as easily as isolate. A unique story that scrutinizes senior cognitive decline, betrayal, aspirations, and, hopefully, reconciliation.

The story is full of emotion, raw, alternately filled with wry bursts of humor. It's written in an intelligent, sensitive, and articulate style that pulls in the reader and doesn't let go. The conclusion is both heartbreaking and tearfully satisfying and is heartily recommended. Not just family drama. Truly literary magic.

—Rosepoint Publishing

COMING SOON

INTERVIEWS

A compilation of Phil Berardelli's most notable encounters during his four-decade-long career as a journalist.

During his years in the media, Phil Berardelli encountered some exceptional people. In this small volume, Phil has compiled his most notable interviews, encompassing distinguished individuals in fields as widely divergent as cinema, public education, microbiology, bioethics and even White House science policy. It represents a small slice of the population of visionaries, people who have contributed to the quality of life, pushed the bounds of achievement and expanded the sphere of human thought. It's a worthwhile collection of interactions – and one lost opportunity – with some of the best minds on the planet.

IMAGINE: Winning the New Cold War

Mountain Lake Press, through its new imprint Legacy Books, proudly announces its most ambitious and important title to date, and the first installment of a planned series on critical public policy issues.

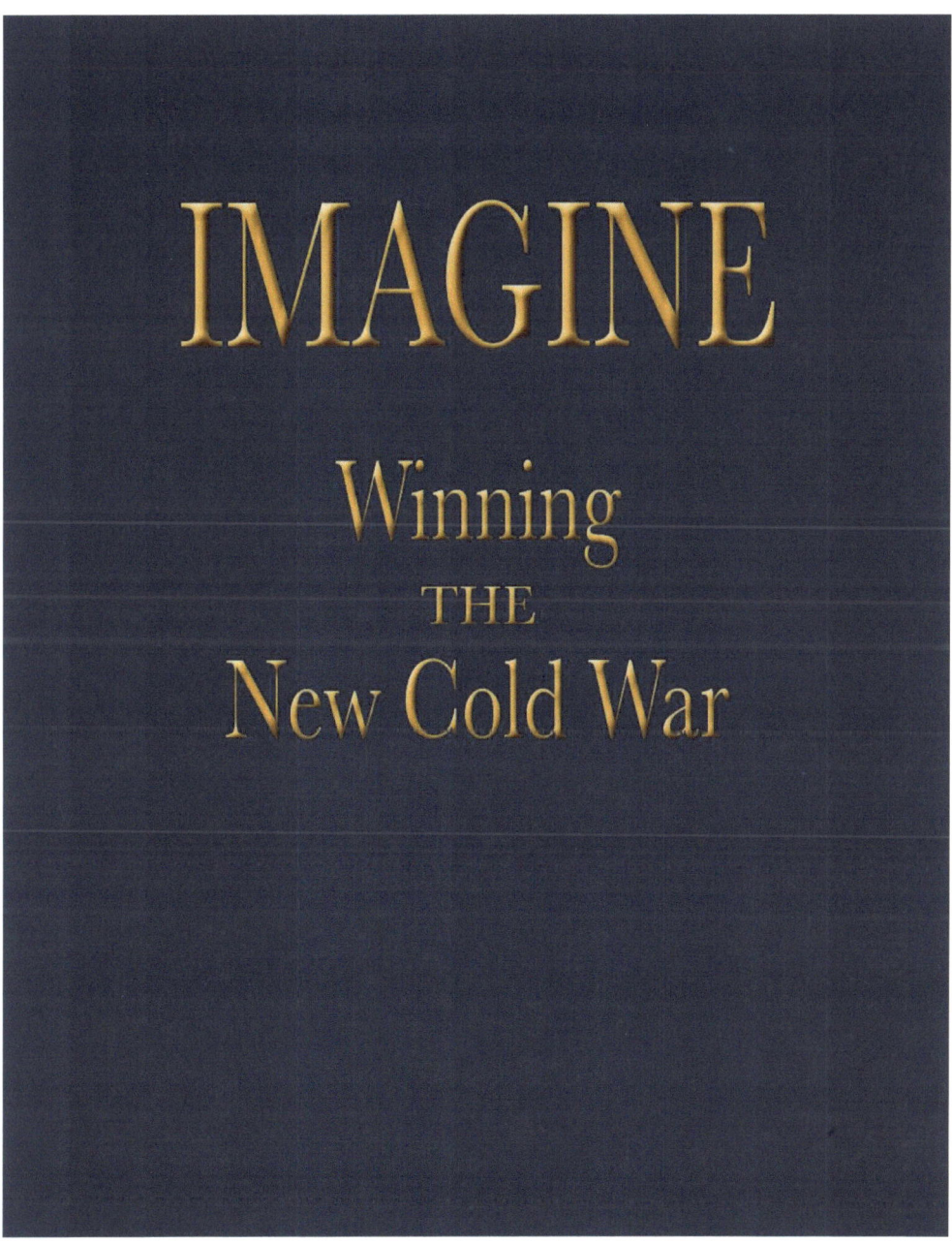

We began with two simple questions: Is the United States now in a new Cold War? If so, what must this country do to prevail? Then we invited 50 distinguished Americans to answer those questions. The result is one of the most unusual – an valuable – books ever produced on the topic of national security.

Each of the 50, former senior members of the intelligence community, the military, the foreign service and the executive branch, with several outstanding representatives from academia, weighs in with his or her own unique brand of expertise. Their collective purpose: to advise, from their current positions as citizens and patriots, the next iteration of the country's national security leadership on ways in which the United States can win this new Cold War that has emerged between our country and its allies, and the axis comprising the People's Republic of China, the Russian Federation, the Islamic Republic of Iran and the Democratic People's Republic of (North) Korea.

That advice is surprisingly diverse – not that any one of the writers doubts that America is under threat from those four adversaries. Rather, the diversity lies in the approaches to victory. Some offer highly technical and precise recommendations, while others recommend broad reforms that promise to, as the saying goes, create a rising tide that will life all boats. And some warn that the biggest threat facing our country comes not from outside adversaries but from the wide gulf currently dividing the two main political parties and our citizenry.

Whatever the differences in content, however, the group shares a staunch belief in the resilience of America and its people, and our capacity to overcome even the most serious and dangerous challenges. If there is a single, recurring and unifying theme in this mix of commentaries, it is hopefulness – hopefulness in the American people and the American spirit. The 50 writers create a collective strategy to, indeed, IMAGINE that we can win the new Cold War.

Guardian of the Crossroads

For her sixth novel, Melanie Forde creates yet another vivid assortment of characters, including the heroine, but this time extending into the realm of the supernatural.

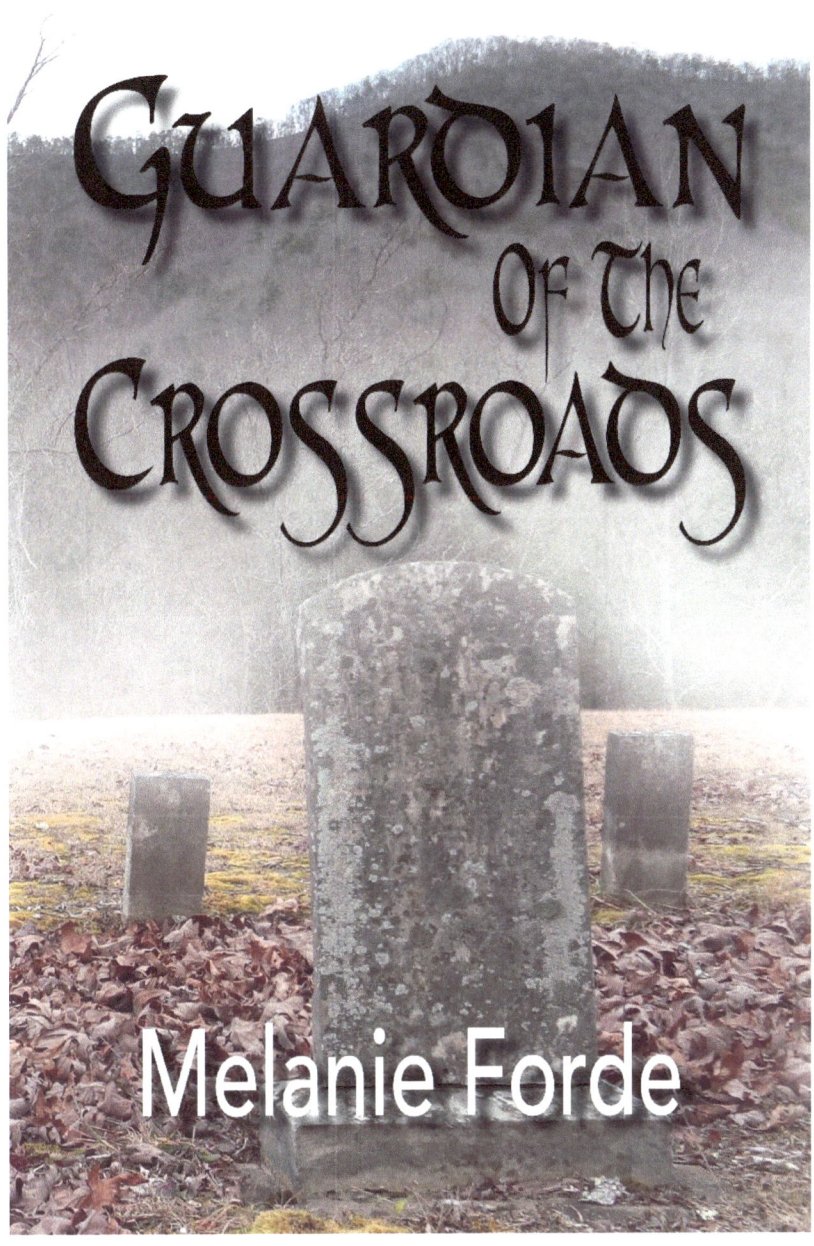

Catherine Devine becomes a minor, local celebrity in Fauquier Country, Virginia, after saving a child from an oncoming truck. Cate is an unlikely heroine. Stuck in a dead-end job as a school crossing guard, she has never chalked up any noteworthy achievement, never had a close friend, never thrilled to romance. After an exhausting decade caring for her dying, demanding mother, she struggles with wobbly health and precarious finances. Stalled in her forties, Cate lacks sufficient faith in herself or the future to craft any plans—grand or small.

Until the her (highly unwelcome) fifteen minutes of fame, Cate has never stood out, with one exception. She occasionally experiences psychokinesis, always accompanied by the embarrassing emission of body fluids, resulting in further social alienation. As she ponders just how she stopped that truck from killing the child, she comes to believe her mind can move more than just physical objects. Perhaps it can move time itself. She considers using that potential to her own advantage. She dives deep within her own consciousness to launch a journey of discovery—perhaps a literal one, perhaps an emotionally intense mental exercise, perhaps a bizarre mid-life crisis. Her time-bending quest doesn't necessarily right old wrongs, but it does offer insights about free will and destiny.

Contributing to that quest are Ruth Levine, a sixty-something school teacher whose maternal streak is counterbalanced by a dollop of wry unconventionality; the flamboyant Morwenna Della Grazia, grade-school teacher and self-styled Wiccan; the well-grounded Roy Washington, caretaker at the estate where Cate rents the gatehouse; Nicu Radulescu, a bullied, creative, whip-smart nine-year-old; Aaron Rappaport, nerdy school chum turned tech mogul; and Lassiter Brown, Cate's weary psychotherapist.

Cate's constant companion on her journey is her faithful wolfhound, Hecuba, an old soul who has always considered her mistress someone very, very special—perhaps even a goddess.

The Human Drama

Jessie Thorpe's intriguing third novel begins two years before the Millennium and involves characters living in the Washington, D.C., area, within – but not necessarily involved in – the city's sphere of politics.

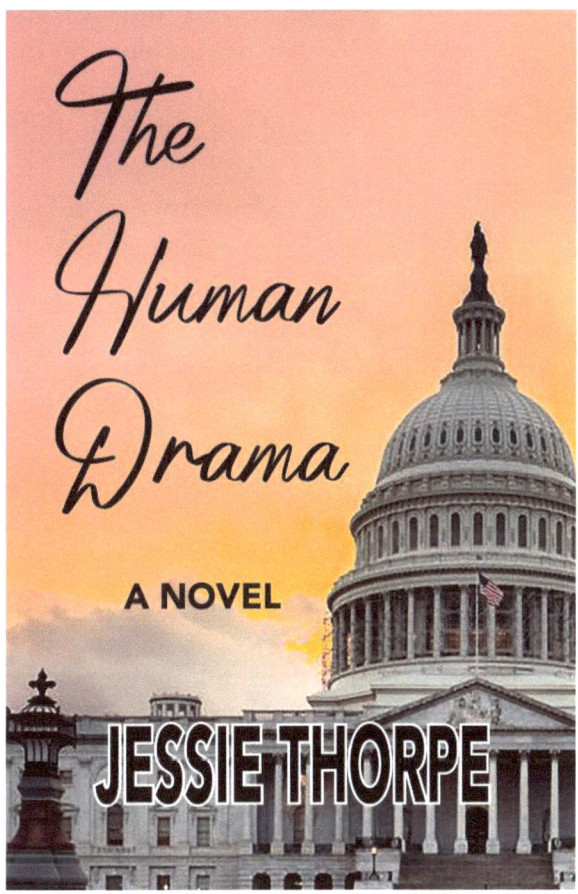

In ***The Human Drama***, lives interconnect and encompass the nation's capital's rich mix of power and ambition and failure. Reality and appearances are in stark contrast—with money at the root of it all.

The characters struggle with small problems and human failings—all the while trying to touch greatness. It seems possible in a place like D.C. Steve and Pauline Denton look like winners. They are attractive and charming. They possess a kind of confidence you almost have to be born with. They make life look simple and fun.

Before the Dentons "moved up," they lived in a neighborhood near Neel and Jenna Guenther. Good friends, the friendship survived the move, and the couples get together frequently.

The Dentons' lives are—complicated? Enhanced?—by the fact that Neel's father lives with them. He is Harmon Guenther, a two-term former congressman from Wisconsin. His service was many years ago. He has retained a few connections and was able to secure Neel's job for him, one of many sources of conflict between the two men. Harmon is in his mid-eighties and needs some care for physical problems. But he still is fully in charge of his faculties and is almost cannily aware of what goes on around him. He "speaks his mind" with unbearable directness.

Jenna treats him with quiet respect but is rather worn out with his needs at times. Neel keeps a distance, using Jenna as a buffer. Although Neel is 42 and Jenna is 34, the two feel tired much of the time.

Other characters include extended family members and colleagues at work. But this is not a typical "Washington Novel," in the sense of being concerned with White House or congressional scandals. Politics loom only in the background. In **The Human Drama**, the characters reside in an outer circle, a slight remove from the power struggles and the aura of importance and ambition that define the city. The battles fought are not between parties and ideologies but the personal ones of trying to hang on and get ahead or get somewhere. At the heart of these lives are waste, insecurity and fear but also joy in life in all its utter complexity.

As she did with her first two acclaimed novels, Jessie Thorpe is crafting a sharply focused character study. But instead of a single, unforgettable individual such as Brook Roper, the protagonist of *Bolton Roper*; or the tortured, ultimately heartbreaking affair between Jack Bridges and Nina Talbott in *Mr. Bridges*, she is training her deeply insightful literary gifts on a larger assortment of individuals. In what could be considered her most absorbing narrative yet, Jessie Thorpe again shows why her work is often called "extraordinary."

Phil's 2001 Nights at the Movies

A collection of, as the title suggests, more than two thousand capsule reviews by a writer with a gift for making clear and compelling arguments for – and against – choosing a movie for your evening's entertainment.

Over a 10-year period, Phil Berardelli compiled three volumes of 500 favorite movies each. Now, expanding that process, Phil adds 501 new titles – though not necessarily favorites or even worth watching. The combined effort comprises a unique compendium of cinema history and a compact but invaluable addition to every home video library.

OUR AUTHORS

Luke Bencie

Among Enemies: Counter-Espionage for the Business Traveler

Global Security Consulting: How to Build a Thriving International Practice

For nearly 30 years, **Luke Bencie** has traveled to more than 140 countries on behalf of the U.S. intelligence community, as well as for the private defense industry. He has experienced – firsthand and sometimes painfully – the threat of espionage. He has seen the lengths to which foreign intelligence services and other hostile global competitors will go to steal American business secrets. Mr. Bencie currently serves as Managing Director of Security Management International, LLC, a security-consulting firm in the Washington, D.C., area. A native of Detroit and a graduate of Michigan State University and The George Washington University's Elliott School of International Affairs, he frequently lectures to defense contractors, U.S. government agencies and Fortune 500 companies on how to protect themselves and their intellectual property from espionage while traveling abroad. He lives on the Gulf Coast of Florida.

Phil Berardelli

Drive On! Preserve and Prolong Your Time on the Road (editor)

The Driving Challenge: Dare to Be Safer and Happier on the Road

In the Stars: Cosmic Reports and Commentary

Phil's Favorite 500: Loves of a Moviegoing Lifetime

Phil's 2nd Favorite 500: More Loves of a Moviegoing Lifetime

Phil's 3rd Favorite 500: Still More Loves of a Moviegoing Lifetime

Safe Young Drivers: A Guide for Parents and Teens

Save Gas? Drive Safe!

Phil Berardelli is the Publisher of Mountain Lake Press. Previously, for 40 years, he worked as a journalist covering such topics as energy policy, popular culture, highway safety and science. His work has appeared in The Washington Post, Washington Times, Los Angeles Times, Pittsburgh Post-Gazette and many other newspapers and magazines. He has served as an editor for McGraw-Hill, TIME-LIFE and United Press International. Born in Pittsburgh, Pennsylvania, he has lived in Northern Virginia since 1970 and in the endless hills of western Maryland since 2012.

R.A. Comunale

Requiem for the Bone Man: A Novel

The Legend of Safehaven: A Novel

Clover: A Dr. Galen Novel

Berto's World: Stories

Dr. Galen's Little Black Bag: Stories

Galen's 30

R.A. Comunale, who died in 2023 after a long illness, was a physician who maintained a family practice and aviation medicine specialty for half a century out of his home/office in McLean, Virginia. Also during his tenure, he enjoyed writing, gardening, collecting antiques, pounding on his piano and yelling at his succession of dimwitted cats. He considered himself an eccentric and iconoclast.

Melanie Forde

Hillwilla: A Novel

On the Hillwilla Road: A Novel

Reinventing Hillwilla: A Novel

Decanted Truths: A Novel

The Quarryman's Girl: A Novel

Melanie Forde is a veteran writer who has ghosted in diverse formats, from academic white papers to advertising copy. Under her own name, she has published numerous features and commentaries about the natural world. Fond of parsing the mysteries of Mother Nature, the former city girl has undertaken such foolhardy challenges as turning flax seed into linen over the course of many labor-intense months. "Never again!" she declares. Ms. Forde really did live on a West Virginia farm, but with two dogs, one cat, and a husband.

Tawfik Hamid

Inside Jihad: How Radical Islam Works, Why It Should Terrify Us, How to Defeat It

Dr. Tawfik Hamid is considered a world authority on Islamism and counterterrorism. A former jihadist, he has been a keynote speaker at intelligence summits in Washington, D.C., and elsewhere. He has discussed jihadism with senators and members of Congress and has lectured at conferences on the topic and at several universities. He has been featured on Fox News, CNN and the BBC, and he has published analyses in *The Wall Street Journal*, the *National Review* and for the Hudson Institute.

Richard L. Holm

The Craft We Chose: My Life in the CIA

Richard L. Holm is a former paramilitary adviser, operations officer, senior manager and chief of station for the Central Intelligence Agency. He is the recipient of a special achievement award for his service in Southeast Asia; the Donovan Award for his work at CIA headquarters in Langley, Virginia; the Distinguished Intelligence Medal, the highest award the agency can bestow; and the Hugh Montgomery Award for career service, bestowed in 2012 for only the second time by the O.S.S. Society. He lives in Northern Virginia.

Richard Phillip Lawless

Hunting Nukes: A Fifty-Year Pursuit of Atomic Bomb Builders and Mischief Makers

Richard Phillip Lawless was born in Peoria, Illinois, in 1946 and matriculated at the University of Missouri, Bradley University and the U.S. Defense Language Institute in Monterey, California. He served in Asia with U.S. Army counterintelligence from 1967 to 1970 then joined the Central Intelligence Agency in 1972, there serving in the Directorate of Operations for 15 years. In this capacity he was posted in Seoul, Vienna, Tokyo, and Washington. He completed his CIA career as a special project manager for Director William Casey. In 2002, in the wake of 9/11, Lawless returned to U.S. government service within the policy component of the Department of Defense, serving as the Deputy Undersecretary of Defense for Asian and Pacific Security Affairs. During this five-year period, working with and for Defense Secretaries Donald Rumsfeld and Robert Gates, he also served as the deputy head of the U.S. delegation to the Beijing Six-Party Talks, which dealt with the North Korean nuclear issue. He resides with his wife Mimi in Northern Virginia, where he remains active in national security consulting and technology innovation.

André Le Gallo

The Caliphate

Satan's Spy

The Red Cell

During his lengthy career with the Central Intelligence Agency, **André Le Gallo** – who passed away in 2017 after a long illness – weathered several coups, a war, and a revolution, working across three continents. He served in operations that ranged from the sensitive to the extremely dangerous, holding senior positions and engaging frequently in some of the most challenging actions to protect his country from its enemies. Le Gallo's novels reflect the extensive knowledge he gained from those experiences, enabling him to produce a suspense trilogy of unparalleled detail.

Charles Long

Adventures in the Scream Trade: Scenes from an Operatic Life

Charles Long has lived an eclectic life. A professional musician and Equity actor before age 20, he became a leading baritone at New York City Opera by age 30, a symphony conductor by age 40, and a published writer by age 45. An Ayn Rand Libertarian, he has testified before various branches of government on civil liberties issues. He also has taught voice, piano and music history at the college level. A lifelong boxing fan, he was a staff writer for the online magazine FightBeat and still contributes commentary and essays for Convicted Artist Magazine. Born in Pittsburgh, Pennsylvania, with a stint in the pristine forests of Washington State, he now resides within the expansive deserts of Arizona.

Jessie Thorpe

Small Wonders: Reviews and Commentary

Bolton Roper: A Novel

Mr. Bridges: A Novel

Jessie Thorpe is Acquisitions Editor for Mountain Lake Press. For 10 years previously she worked as a freelance writer and copy editor, providing research and editorial support for international business concerns. She also worked as a book critic for United Press International. Born in Detroit, Michigan, she has lived in Northern Virginia since 1968 and western Maryland since 2012.

BOOK INFORMATION

Paperbacks

TITLE	ISBN	No. of Pages
*Adventures in the Scream Trade***	978-1-959307-24-2	200
*Among Enemies***	978-1-732429-72-7	153***
*Berto's World***	978-0-981477-32-9	213
*Bolton Roper**	978-1-959307-08-2	338
*The Caliphate**	978-1-959307-26-6	440
*Clover***	978-0-984651-20-7	208
*The Craft We Chose***	978-1-959307-25-9	584***
*Decanted Truths**	978-1-959307-02-0	390
*Dr. Galen's Little Black Bag***	978-0-981477-35-0	202
*Drive On!**	978-1-959307-12-9	192
*The Driving Challenge**	978-1-959307-11-2	194
*Galen's 30**	978-1-959307-40-2	189
*Global Security Consulting**	978-1-732429-73-4	281***
*Hillwilla**	978-1-959307-07-5	264
*Hunting Nukes**	978-1-959307-36-5	490***
In the Stars	978-1-959307-37-2	172
*Inside Jihad**	978-0-990808-91-6	240***
*The Legend of Safehaven***	978-1-981477-33-6	248
*Mr. Bridges**	978-1-959307-20-4	310
*On the Hillwilla Road**	978-1-959307-06-8	280
*Phil's Favorite 500**	978-1-959307-14-3	544
*Phil's 2nd Favorite 500**	978-1-959307-16-7	472
*Phil's 3rd Favorite 500**	978-1-959307-18-1	472
*The Quarryman's Girl**	978-1-959307-00-6	281
*The Red Cell**	978-1-959307-30-3	289
*Reinventing Hillwilla**	978-1-959307-04-4	313

Requiem for the Bone Man**	978-1-981477-30-5	248
*Safe Young Drivers**	978-1-959307-10-5	192***
*Satan's Spy**	978-1-959307-28-0	411
*Save Gas? Drive Safe!**	978-1-959307-13-6	86
*Small Wonders**	978-1-959307-22-8	213

* Ebook edition available   **Ebook and audiobook editions available ***Indexed

Hardcovers/Casewraps

TITLE	ISBN	No. of Pages
*Adventures in the Scream Trade**	978-0-981477-34-3	200
*Among Enemies**	978-0-988591-91-2	153***
*Bolton Roper**	978-1-959307-09-9	338
*The Caliphate**	978-1-959307-27-3	440
*The Craft We Chose**	978-0-981477-37-4	584***
*Decanted Truths**	978-1-959307-03-7	390
*Galen's 30****	978-1-959307-41-9	189
*Global Security Consulting**	978-1-990808-90-9	281***
*Hillwilla**	978-0-988591-97-4	264
*Hunting Nukes**	978-1-959307-39-6	490***
*In the Stars**	978-1-959307-38-9	172
*Mr. Bridges**	978-1-959307-21-1	310
*On the Hillwilla Road**	978-0-9908-8-93-0	280
*Phil's Favorite 500**	978-1-959307-15-0	543
*Phil's 2nd Favorite 500**	978-1-959307-17-4	472
*Phil's 3rd Favorite 500**	978-1-959307-19-8	472
*The Quarryman's Girl**	978-1-959307-01-3	281
*The Red Cell**	978-1-959307-31-0	289
*Reinventing Hillwilla**	978-1-959307-05-1	313
*Satan's Spy**	978-1-959307-29-7	411
*Small Wonders**	978-1-959307-23-5	213

* Released in formal hardcover **Casewrap edition only ***Indexed